PEASANT POLITICS

PEASANT POLITICS
Conflict and Development in Murang'a

Geoff Lamb

ST. MARTIN'S PRESS · NEW YORK

Copyright © 1974 by Geoff Lamb
All rights reserved. For information, write:
St. Martin's Press, Inc., 175 Fifth Avenue, New York, N.Y. 10010
Library of Congress Catalog Card Number: 74-77270
Printed in Great Britain
First published in the United States of America in 1974

AFFILIATED PUBLISHERS: Macmillan Limited, London
also at Bombay, Calcutta, Madras and Melbourne

CONTENTS

	FOREWORD	vii
	ABBREVIATIONS	x
	PREFACE	xi
I	INTRODUCTION	1
II	THE POLITICS OF INDEPENDENCE	17
III	POLITICAL CONFLICT IN MURANG'A	28
IV	DEVELOPMENT AND LOCAL POLITICS: THE ROLE OF THE COMMUNITY DEVELOPMENT OFFICER	54
V	COFFEE AND AGRICULTURAL DEVELOPMENT	83
VI	COFFEE, CO-OPERATIVES AND POLITICS	110
VII	POWER, DEVELOPMENT AND POLITICAL CHANGE	132
	APPENDIX	153

for BARBARA

FOREWORD

During the 1960s empirical studies of politics in Africa passed through a frequently unrewarding phase. The general perspective which informed many if not most of them was that of regimes in power—both those of the third world and those of the 'aid donor' countries (from which the majority of political researchers came). This perspective presupposed that the central issue of politics was one of facilitating the process of 'development', conceived essentially as rapidly expanded output per head, by means of a parallel process of 'political development'. But the nature of this latter process remained unclear, in spite of elaborate attempts to specify it; and at the level of empirical enquiry that this orientation was apt to produce were studies of the *mechanisms of rule*—party organization, 'development administration', managed elections, etc—from which the stuff of politics—conflict, struggle, and, above all, the historical significance of the issues at stake—had often been largely excluded.

This phase of African political studies has at least been punctuated—though not terminated—primarily as a result of the failure of most African and other third world economies to 'develop' to the extent that had been hoped, and of the increasingly apparent connexion between this fact and the nature of the domestic and foreign interests which the various regimes in question actually represent. Although it would be a mistake to suppose that the bulk of research on third world politics was becoming detached from the standpoint of these interests, there has been a revival of concern with politics proper, and with the historical significance of the progressive polarization of politics throughout the third world.

Geoff Lamb's study of the interaction of 'local politics' and 'development administration' in a single district of Kenya in 1967 is a contribution to this much-needed change of direction, and in the context of Africa, an early one. In a few African countries, and notably in Ghana and Tanzania, regimes in power in the 1960s posed fundamental challenges to the interests of foreign capital, giving rise to debates which stimulated some valuable empirical research on the social formations bequeathed by colonialism, the nature of the political struggles taking place within them, and the bearing of these on the prospects for a break with foreign dependency and a transition to socialism. But elsewhere in Africa, and especially in English-speaking countries, field work bearing on these questions was exceptional. The present study would therefore be valuable if it did no more than report, as it does, the political life of a particular locality in Kenya in the mid-1960s in such a way as to relate it to these themes. In this book, development policy and its administration—in the shape of Community Development, the control of coffee production and the control of co-operatives—can be seen to be aspects of the subordination of the Kenyan economy to the interests of foreign capital, i.e. aspects of 'blocked' development, or underdevelopment; and 'local-level politics' appears (though this is a slight gloss on the text, as will be indicated in a moment) as an aspect of the struggle for ascendency between strata of embryonic social classes, or fractions of existing classes. The author does not conceal the complexity of events, or deny the reality of the various forms in which both the 'development of underdevelopment' and nascent class struggles were manifested: planning and administrative structures, factionalism, clientelism, etc. But the narrative keeps in view the fact that what actually happened in each field of 'development policy' studied was largely the result of a continuing and mainly successful struggle by the 'rich peasant' farmers, in alliance with smaller landholders, first against the poor and landless supporters of the opposition party, then against foreign estate capital on the issue of coffee acreages; and finally, against the central bureaucracy, at the expense of the smaller producers, on the issue of who should control the co-operative societies' funds. And the concluding chapter raises a number of centrally important questions for the future development of countries in Africa where similar social forces are at work.

The book largely refrains, however, from proposing definite answers to these questions, even as regards Kenya, or even the district of Murang'a, mainly on the grounds that the evidence is still incomplete. While this is true, the question also arises whether the terms of the analysis have yet been adequately formulated, and whether a theoretical advance, rather than the accumulation of further data, is not the essential next step. What is at issue here can be illustrated by considering the treatment of the different elements of Murang'a society in this study. As the author says, 'class formation and related patterns of political power' play a central part in his story, yet his use of concepts for the analysis of these phenomena is eclectic; in particular, the people who dominated Murang'a politics are rarely described as a class, or part of a class, but variously as a 'rural leadership', a 'peasant elite', 'wealthier peasants', etc., although on the evidence presented they were very conscious of their class interests, and defended them effectively. So the question is: is the difficulty due, as the author suggests, to lack of evidence about the long-term consequences of the events reported in this book, or is the lack of an adequate theoretical framework determining the apparent inconclusiveness of the evidence?

It seems to me that the second alternative is truer than the first, and that further progress depends on certain theoretical conditions being met. First, the class character of political groups or social categories cannot be discovered from their political activities or the distribution of income and assets, but requires a systematic analysis of the modes of production (and their interconnexion or articulation) on which the class structure is based. This kind of analysis has still to be carried out, not only for Kenya but for most parts of the third world. Second, in analysing the class structure of a given social formation we must be less concerned to assign this or that category or group to its correct general class, than to grasp the historical development of the various strata and fractions of single classes, and the alliances and antagonisms between these, as well as the basic antagonisms between classes. Last but not least, the analysis of a society in terms of its classes discloses structures of exploitation and oppression about which it is impossible to remain neutral; to make the analysis consistent the researcher is, I think, obliged to clarify his commitments, often a difficult and painful matter.

To say that this book poses very clearly the question which has just been discussed might seem at first sight to be a rather back-handed compliment, yet the view which I have expressed, and which seems to differ from the author's, is one towards which his own work has helped to impel me. And in fact it seems to me that the value of his book consists not only in what it clearly establishes, but also in the unresolved questions, many of them critical for everyone concerned with the problems of the third world, which it represents in a very concrete way.

Colin Leys

ABBREVIATIONS

CBK	Coffee Board of Kenya
CD	Community Development
CDA	Community Development Assistant
CDO	Community Development Officer
CEO	County Education Officer
DAO	District Agricultural Officer
DC	District Commissioner
DO	District Officer
ICA	International Coffee Agreement
KADU	Kenya African Democratic Union
KANU	Kenya African National Union
KAU	Kenya African Union
KCA	Kikuyu Central Association
KEM	Kikuyu, Embu and Meru
KPU	Kenya People's Union
TANU	Tanzania African National Union
UNICEF	United Nations Children's Fund

PREFACE

Murang'a District begins about 30 miles north of Nairobi in Kenya's Central Province. It is almost wholly Kikuyu, bounded on the south by Kiambu District and on the north by Nyeri and Kirinyaga Districts (all three of them Kikuyu districts), on the west by the Nyandarua range of mountains, and on the east by the Kamba district of Machakos. Its population is overwhelmingly African: the 1969 census registered 444,300 Kenyan Africans, 510 Asians and 269 Europeans. With this population, and a land area of 2,529 square kilometers, Murang'a was in 1969 the fourth most densely populated rural district in Kenya out of a total of just under 40—the district had an average density of 176 people per square kilometer.[1]

Ecological zones run roughly in north-south parallels: a high altitude zone near the Nyandarua forests, with bracken the predominant natural vegetation, a middle-level star grass zone which is extremely fertile and supports two maize crops a year, and an easterly drier zone which is much less densely populated and which at its easternmost extremities supports only grazing and a small amount of cotton. The district is divided laterally by very steep ridges and deep valleys running roughly east-west, with cultivation mainly on the flat ridge tops and hillside terraces.

The major cash crop is coffee, which earned about £2 million for the district in 1972. Other cash crops have been of relatively small value, although tea, dairy products and to a lesser extent macadamia nuts play a growing role in the district economy. Aside from coffee and these subsidiary crops, wattle, pyrethrum, sisal and pineapples are grown for export outside district boundaries, while the main crops for subsistence and local sale are maize, beans and bananas.

Murang'a town, the district headquarters (formerly known, as was the district itself, as Fort Hall), lies on the main rail and road routes between Nairobi and the more northerly centres of Nyeri, Nanyuki and

---

[1] *Kenya Population Census 1969,* Vol. 1. Statistics Division, Ministry of Finance and Economic Planning, November 1970. The figures include Makuyu Division of the district, which consists mainly of European estates, and which thus has a population density of only 59 people per square kilometre, while density in the other divisions is much higher: Kigumo 132, Kiharu 226, Kangema 251 and Kandara 302.

Isiolo; these communications run along the eastern side of the district, however, and communications to the west have only in the last few years begun to improve with the government's expanded roads programme and in particular with the development of tea growing in the western uplands of the district.

Research for this book, which is based on a doctoral dissertation for the University of Sussex, was carried out mainly during a stay in Murang'a for some seven months in 1967. Further information on Murang'a politics was gained during a trip to Kenya in 1971-72, in the course of a separate but related research project. I owe a debt of gratitude to scores of Murang'a people who put up so courteously with my inquisitiveness. I am particularly grateful to Mr Wilson Wahome, Community Development Officer, who not only answered innumerable questions, but arranged accommodation for my wife and myself, introduced me to the official community, and was always ready to give advice and help; to the District Commissioner, Mr Charles Karoga Koinange and his successor, Mr J. M. Tiampati; to the District Agricultural Officer, Mr Douglas Kahuthia, and Mr P. G. M. Kathendu, Co-operative Officer; to Mr Geoffrey Kebatta, secretary-manager of Murang'a Farmers' Co-operative Union Ltd.; Mr Zephania Muhia of the County Council staff; Messrs Kamau Njoroge, Mwangi Thabuni and Jasmel Kariuki of KANU; and *Mzee* Bildad Kaggia, who gave us much of his time and invaluable information. I must also thank Tony Hall, then Political Correspondent of the Nairobi *Daily Nation,* and his wife Eve, for sharing with me their knowledge of Kenyan politics.

I am grateful to the United Nations Education and Training Programme for South Africans, the University of Sussex, the Institute of Development Studies at Sussex, and Sir Robert Birley, for financial assistance.

Professors Bruce Graham, Bernard Schaffer, William Tordoff and Cherry Gertzel assisted me with their criticisms of parts or the whole of the manuscript through various stages of its writing: I am very grateful for their help. The faults and shortcomings in these pages are of course purely my own.

Chapter I

INTRODUCTION

This book is a study of political conflict in a peasant community. It examines the way in which the political leaders of Murang'a District fought over power, wealth and status in the first years of independence, and tries to assess how, in the course of these struggles, these peasant leaders affected the distribution not only of political power but of economic resources in the Murang'a countryside. The central questions being asked can thus be set out very simply—deceptively so, for the simple questions about politics are often the most important, and the most complicated to answer. How did Murang'a politicians influence the central government in the directions they desired? Within the district, which sections of the population benefited from rural development and which did not, and why? How important was political power at the local level in determining the distribution of economic benefits and burdens?

It will be clear that the answers to such questions involve political processes and structures which are not confined to a single rural district: indeed, the emphasis throughout is upon the complex interactions between centre and locality, upon the 'variety of peasant adaptations to the growth of the private enterprise money economy'.[1] In the analysis of these interactions, and of the nature of power relationships within Murang'a itself, conclusions will thus be drawn about the social basis of political conflict, about the character of the national elite, its perceptions and priorities, and its relationship with the peasant hinterland—in short, about the trajectory of Kenyan politics. The discussion in this context will find little common ground with the American-influenced writing about African politics which

---

[1] Colin Leys, 'Politics in Kenya: the development of peasant society'. *British Journal of Political Science,* Vol. 1, No. 1, 1971.

predominated during much of the Sixties[2]; it attempts, however, to contribute to current debates on the direction of African politics,[3] to the study of peasant politics[4] and, tangentially, the political economy of underdevelopment.[5]

The study of course concentrates on events at a very lowly point in the international structure of which Kenya is a part, and there is no attempt to examine all the ties connecting Murang'a with the national and international systems—nor for that matter to examine all the lines spreading downwards, as it were, to the peasant base of the structure. Nevertheless the complexity of interaction is readily apparent. The coffee economy and therefore the economic basis for factional politics in the district is affected and partially sustained by buyers from London or Hamburg as well as by the powerholders in Nairobi; the maintenance of unrestricted access to state resources for the educational elite may well be necessary to safeguard the continued inflow of investment funds into Kenya, and is almost certainly central to the avoidance of an unemployed intelligentsia and hence the possible politicization of discontent; population pressure in the rural areas may in future dictate the takeover of further substantial areas of white-owned land, necessitating action not only domestically, but by overseas aid agencies and governments; and so on. These structures may not be seen as of central importance in everyday political life in Murang'a, and the perception of them by the local actors involved may be partial or

---

[2] The *locus classicus* of this approach as applied to the Third World is, of course, the Introduction to Almond and Coleman's *Politics of the Developing Areas* (Princeton, Princeton University Press, 1960). The arguments there expounded have been much revised and refined (notably in Almond's later work); the basic intellectual approach persists, however, and the ideological underpinnings seem to become more apparent the more their existence is denied.

[3] See for example Giovanni Arrighi and John Saul, 'Socialism and Economic Development in Tropical Africa', *Journal of Modern African Studies,* Vol. 6, No. 2, 1968; Leys op. cit.; Ruth First, *The Barrel of a Gun: Political Power in Africa and the Coup d'Etat* (London, Allen Lane the Penguin Press, 1970); and studies linked more specifically to individual territories, such as those of Samir Amin on the Maghreb and the Ivory Coast, Basil Davidson on Guine-Bissau, and many others. Ruth First's book provides a useful survey of the literature.

[4] For example Eric R. Wolf, *Peasants* (Prentice-Hall, 1966); Barrington Moore, *Social Origins of Dictatorship and Democracy* (Harmondsworth, Peregrine Books, 1969); Hamza Alavi, 'Peasants and Revolution', in R. Millibrand and John Savile, eds., *Socialist Register 1964* (London, Merlin Press); and the collection by Teodor Shanin, *Peasants and Peasant Societies* (Harmondsworth, Penguin Books, 1971) See especially in this collection the article by John Saul and Roger Woods, 'African Peasantries'.

[5] On this theme in a specifically East African context, see the study by E. A. Brett, *Colonialism and Underdevelopment: Britain in East Africa 1918-1939* (London, Heinemann, 1973).

intermittent: nevertheless they form the framework which gives local conflict a wider significance, and will be referred to in later chapters in analysing the way in which Murang'a politicians are related to the world outside the district.

The metaphors of conflict and incorporation, therefore, are those most relevant to this study. Thus, for example, the themes of the Kenyan version of African Socialism[6] are discussed less in terms of the 'presumptive solidarity and ... automatically socialist "attitude of mind" '[7] which that document, like much other African theorizing about socialism, assumes to exist in African society, and more in terms of the distribution of resources which it implies, and the effect of such distribution on social conflict in the countryside. Equally, it seems that the ruling party, KANU, in Murang'a and in Kenya as a whole, made much less sense as a mobilizing agent, for example (which it is often claimed to be), than as a convenient mechanism for co-opting oppositional elements, for distributing patronage, and for regulating entry into the elite political arena. Here, as might be expected, there is a debt to what is rather arbitrarily called political anthropology, and especially to the work of F. G. Bailey, Ralph W. Nicholas and B. D. Graham.[8]

Kenya represented an advanced stage in the penetration of colonial African economies by metropolitan capital. Nairobi acted as the commercial and industrial focus for the whole of East Africa from the Twenties onwards; but even more importantly, the colonization of vast areas of land by white settlers created conditions which ensured that Africans—particularly Kikuyu—were drawn into the capitalist economy with a thoroughness which had few parallels in British colonial Africa. Some of the dimensions of this incorporation are obvious—for example the quite rapid monetarization of the Kikuyu economy (and those of other Kenyan African areas to a lesser extent) by the imposition of taxes and of agricultural labour requirements, and (much later) by opportunities for Africans to grow crops for cash. As a result of these and other influences, marked structural discontinuity between centre and locality is not a feature of Murang'a politics. But the precise consequences of this process of colonial and neo-colonial change are much harder to assess, even if the economic and political outcomes at

---

[6] *African Socialism and its Application to Planning in Kenya,* Sessional Paper No. 10, 1965 (Nairobi, Government Printer, 1965).
[7] Arrighi and Saul, op. cit., p. 165.
[8] See especially Bailey's *Stratagems and Spoils* (Oxford, Basil Blackwell, 1969); Nicholas' 'Factions: A Comparative Analysis,' in Michael Banton, ed., *Political Systems and the Distribution of Power* (London, Tavistock Publications, 1965); and Graham's contribution on Indian factionalism in Marc J. Swartz, ed., *Local-level Politics* (University of London Press, 1969).

the national level are broadly clear. It is difficult to gauge, for instance, what kinds of structures and relationships are emerging at the local level? How much autonomy or control over local resources do rural communities possess? What are the mechanisms whereby these resources are exploited and distributed? What are the key external structures involved in the process of rural social and economic change? The model of incorporation suggested by Frank[9] and others, in the main based on the Latin American experience, needs to be rather subtly defined in terms of the contemporary relevance of the specifically Kenyan colonial experience. Thus the characterization of 'peripheral capitalist societies' by a sociologist whose position is close to Frank's:

> 1. *Low interdependence*: the society is divided into localized primary-producing segments having a low rate of exchange with one another.
>
> 2. *External orientation*: the rate of interchange between segments within the same national society is low relative to the rate of interchange between these segments and external units.
>
> 3. *Appendage functions*: external exchange is almost exclusively with the industrialized capitalisms of Euro-America; localized segments serve less as complementary components of a national society than as appendages supplying primary products and profits to metropolitan economies.[10]

The relevance of this sort of analysis to Kenya is plain—but so is the necessity for key modifications which have important implications both for the structure of politics and for the nature of Kenyan economic change. One might point to the fact, for example, that in Kenya the national elite and the capital city itself may be in one sense 'external units', but very closely connected by ties of power and patronage, as also by trade and labour migration patterns. Again, the very lack of development in much of Kenya means that many areas have very few ties either with other localities or with the international economy: the range of options for them is thus theoretically wider than for areas already exporting a primary product, but in practice perhaps more problematical because of the constellation of internal and external constraints on 'latecomers' gaining access to markets or development resources.

In short, Kenya's backwardness introduces important variations

---

[9] See for example his *Capitalism and Underdevelopment in Latin America* (Monthly Review Press, New York, 1967).
[10] Philip Ehrensaft, 'Semi-Industrial Capitalism in the Third World: Implications for Social Research in Africa' (University of Dar es Salaam (mimeo), January 1972).

on the 'development of underdevelopment'—many of which are perhaps not yet perceptible. This is especially true in considering patterns of social stratification and the development of capitalist relationships in the rural areas—and here, as has been elaborated on particularly in the concluding chapter, it may be most valuable to consider whether emerging styles of political conflict are a portent of social changes whose precise nature and extent are as yet unclear. At the same time, it is hoped that the light thrown on political conflict in Murang'a will also illuminate some of the basic development choices facing Kenya as the country responds to international and domestic pressures. Thus, for example, the huge expansion in peasant agricultural output in Kenya over the last fifteen years or so has not only transformed the lives of thousands of individual families; it has also helped to make possible advances in education, in health and nutrition. At the same time, the distribution of these benefits is obviously crucial: agricultural expansion has set in train or accelerated processes of social stratification which might be expected to develop along lines experienced in the past by other capitalist societies.

At this point, however, Kenya's current position in the international economy, itself in part a legacy of the colonial past, becomes highly relevant. On the one hand it seems impossible for peasant agriculture to improve its share of total marketed agricultural output (stagnant, indeed declining very slightly, since 1967, and currently around 48%)[11] without challenging certain basic features of the country's economic environment—notably agricultural export policy, and the advantageous economic and political position of the large farm sector.[12] Equally, the social and political outcome of growing inequality in the rural areas is for the present uncertain: it has been argued by Colin Leys,[13] among others, that stratification and inequality are being accommodated within *peasant* rather than capitalist structures, and hence are being incorporated within the existing Kenyan political system rather than posing a threat to it.

Some of these points will be considered more fully in the concluding chapter, in the light of the Murang'a experience: indeed the course of Murang'a politics in the Sixties bears very directly on these issues, as also on the political development of Kenya as a whole. The remainder

---

[11] *Economic Survey 1971*, Government Printer Nairobi, p. 60.
[12] Gary Wasserman, 'The Politics of Adaption: Kenya European Farmers and the Land Issue, 1960-63'. Universities of East Africa Social Science Council conference papers, 1970, Dar es Salaam. This paper has a good discussion of the international importance of the large farms as a symbol of financial orthodoxy, and of the way in which this view was largely accepted by the incoming African government.
[13] Leys, op. cit.

of this introduction will try to sketch, necessarily in broad strokes, the historical context in which contemporary Murang'a politics must be seen.

The Nationalist Response

By the end of the Twenties, the patterns of modern nationalist politics were already apparent in Kenya, scarcely a quarter of a century after colonial rule had been finally established. For the Kikuyu in particular, the political choices seemed clear-cut: substantial tracts of land had been alienated by whites and, even more importantly, the Kikuyu Reserve had been encircled wherever there had been room for expansion, by white farms. The Kikuyu were thus effectively sealed off to multiply, further to subdivide their already eroding holdings, and to export labour to the settler farms of the Rift Valley. The struggle with the Administration and with the settlers had already been joined over particular issues—land, wage cuts, the *kipande* (pass) system—and the people had begun to learn, during the 'Thuku troubles'[14] in particular, of both the effectiveness of modern political organization and the repressive capacity of the colonial state.

If Harry Thuku and his young Kikuyu colleagues provoked the Administration and settlers to violent reaction, however, they also engendered a reaction by those Kikuyu—chiefs especially—who had substantially benefited from colonization. The hostility between Thuku's followers and the Kikuyu Association (the chief-dominated body which the Administration regarded as the 'true' representative of the Kikuyu) was an early manifestation of a basic difference, both in ideology and in political tactics, which was to be significant throughout the colonial period. In part it was a divergence between chiefs and others with a stake in the colonial system, and the poor of Nairobi and the rural areas; later it was to appear as a struggle between the nationalist intellectual elite and radical trade unionist and peasant leaders. The conflict was not always expressed organizationally however; as with the Kenya African Union in the pre-Emergency period, there existed factions within each organization based on the same sort of cleavage. Broadly, the conflict continued to be between those who accepted the inevitability (or at least the persistence for the foreseeable future) of British colonialism, and those whose demands at least implicitly rejected that premise. This cleavage was important at a

---

[14] The unrest, which included a Nairobi general strike and the shooting of a large number of African demonstrators by settlers and police, followed the arrest of Harry Thuku, the pioneer of Kenyan nationalist politics, in March 1922.

number of crisis points in the colonial period: in the female circumcision issue of the late Twenties, in which 'loyal' Kikuyu found themselves aligned with the white front of Administration, settlers and missionaries against their *karing'a* ('pure') compatriots;[15] in the divisions between moderate and radical factions of the Kikuyu Central Association which followed the brief unity produced by the Carter Land Commission hearings of 1931; and most importantly of all, in the period of nationalist agitation after the Second World War.

The political schisms in Kikuyu society were an inchoate response to the pressures of incorporation into the settler and imperial economic systems. Thus in the slump of the Thirties, wage cuts and unemployment led somewhat paradoxically to a growth in African commercial agriculture as the Administration moved to safeguard its revenue. All these factors put more pressure on the crowded Reserves—pressure exacerbated by the decline of the squatter system in the White Highlands. Moreover, government experts were convinced that soil erosion could only be effectively contained by larger, not smaller, units of land. These forces gave added weight to influences already at work in the Kikuyu Reserve.[16]

> In some areas at least, land was becoming scarce, and the necessary adjustments of economic and social relationships were being made to this supremely important change. Holdings were being bought and sold, and a struggle for ownership was developing between the lineage officials traditionally charged with allotment and adjudication, who were endeavouring to set up as landlords, and the individual cultivators, who were seeking emancipation from communal controls. At the same time those peasants who were not members of the locally dominant lineage were coming to be regarded as tenants, and their rights of occupation were becoming increasingly precarious.[17]

There seems to be no way of discovering the extent of this

---

[15] Compare Frantz Fanon's discussion of French efforts to force Algerian women to abandon the veil; '... the colonized found himself defining a principled position with respect to a formerly inert element in the native cultural configuration...' (*Studies in a Dying Colonialism*, New York, Monthly Review Press, 1965, p. 46. This is the English translation of *L'an Cinq de la Revolution Algerienne*.)

[16] See C. C. Wrigley, 'Kenya: The Patterns of Economic Life, 1902-45', in Vincent Harlow and E. M. Chilver, eds., *History of East Africa*, Vol. II, Clarendon Press, Oxford, 1965, pp. 251-257.

[17] Ibid., p. 255.

commercialization of *githaka* land:[18] students of this period are careful not to attempt to quantify their evidence.[19] It is clear, nevertheless, that the breakdown of lineage tenure in the Kikuyu reserve was sufficiently far advanced—more especially in Kiambu District—to arouse some concern among administrators, and indeed to provoke arguments within the colonial bureaucracy about the desirability of a land reform which would abolish *mbari* tenure and institute freehold, transferable tenure in its place.

It is in this process in the Thirties and Forties, with the landlord-and-tenant system it created and the growing army of landless Kikuyu, that there can be seen both the political crisis which provoked the violent confrontation of the Emergency in 1952, and the bitter rift in Kikuyu society which the Emergency itself produced.

Aside from this cleavage between pro-Mau Mau and anti-Mau Mau Kikuyu, we should be equally concerned with the differences within the nationalist ranks in the immediate pre-Emergency period. The tensions within the leadership of the Kenya African Union and within the secret nationalist 'Parliament' at Banana Hill outside Nairobi reflected the different kinds of commitment of peasantry and embryonic bourgeoisie, as Nottingham and Rosberg express it:

> Two generations of rapid social change had accentuated those features of traditional Kikuyu culture that tended to emphasize individualism and self-achievement. In addition, new patterns of social stratification had evolved, based on a combination of education, land and wealth. Among those at the top of the pyramid were the African administrative class, progressive

---

[18] In traditional society, the basic land unit was the *githaka*, owned jointly by the members of a small local lineage, the *mbari*, which was the basic Kikuyu social unit. The *muramati*, head of the lineage, allocated land subject to each son's right to work some land. These sons in turn became heads of segments of the *githaka*, but in practice often broke away and formed new lineages and separate *ithaka*—until the coming of the whites closed the expanding Kikuyu land frontier. With the decline of clan organization, as Middleton has noted, *githaka* land had become not merely a means of livelihood but the foundation of the social system, for it was membership in an *mbari* and rights to *githaka* land which identified a man as a 'proper' member of Kenyan society. See John Middleton, *The Kikuyu and Kamba of Kenya* (London, International African Institute, 1953).

[19] See for example Wrigley, op. cit.; M. P. K. Sorrenson, *Land Reform in the Kikuyu Country* (Oxford University Press, Nairobi, 1967); John Middleton, 'Kenya: Changes in African Life, 1912-1945' in *History of East Africa*, Vol. II; and of course the study by Carl Rosberg and John Nottingham, *The Myth of Mau Mau* (New York, Praeger, 1966). It will be apparent that I have drawn much information from the last mentioned, an invaluable source of facts and insights about Kikuyu life and politics.

farmers, some teachers, and businessmen. Most of these were adherents of a Christian mission. They were people who had clearly benefited from the British presence, and feared the implications of radical political change. Constitutional nationalism was the limit of their political involvement. But for the overwhelming mass of the population, economic anxiety and social frustration had become increasingly prevalent. Yet, though aspiration for change existed, there seemed no immediate prospect for economic or social reform.[20]

In organizational terms, the peasant militants or their representatives controlled, by 1951, the important Nairobi branch of the KAU (through the leadership of Fred Kubai and Bildad Kaggia, the leaders of the East African Trade Union Congress), and many KAU rural branches outside Kiambu District. In the Kikuyu heartland, KAU branches were often run by the organizational nuclei of the old Kikuyu Central Association, kept alive secretly by local nationalists after the organization's proscription in 1940. Their organizational dominance, and the smell of 'subversion' which enfolded many local KAU branches because of the participation of the old guard, were often enough to scare off potential recruits among local elites and mission adherents.[21]

The tensions between revolutionary and 'semi-constitutional' nationalism were never played out: the State of Emergency declared in October 1952 resulted in the imprisonment of leaders of both wings of the movement—indeed, it placed them in the same dock, literally and figuratively—and ensured that the guerrilla struggle was crippled from the beginning by severed lines of supply and shattered organizational structures, and in political terms by relative ideological backwardness and the isolation in the struggle of the Kikuyu and their ethnic kin, the Embu and Meru.

The political developments of the Emergency years, vital though

---

[20] Ibid., p. 242.
[21] I am aware of the potential for argument and confusion in including Nairobi urban activists in the term 'peasant militants'. The whole issue of the existence and nature of an African 'working class' is fraught with analytical problems: what I am concerned to do here is draw attention to the intimate connection, in general social terms and more narrowly in politico-organizational terms, between town and Kikuyu countryside in the immediate pre-Emergency period. One of the forms this took was that of district-of-origin committees in Nairobi, which played a vital communications and propaganda role in spreading revolutionary sentiments in the countryside, as urban workers returned to their homes. These were fascinatingly similar in organization and revolutionary function to the Bolshevik 'back-home clubs' described by Trotsky in his *History of the Russian Revolution* (London, Sphere Books, 1967, Vol. 3, p. 24).

they were, need not be recounted here—they are amply documented elsewhere and are fairly well known.[22] By 1960 Africans had secured constitutional advances ensuring a black majority in the Legislative Council, and with it the implicit assurance of independence. But for the purpose of this narrative much more attention must be paid to the Emergency from another perspective. Aside from the string of constitutional advances, the period between 1952 and 1960 had a profound effect on the social and political structure of Kenya, and of Kikuyu country in particular. Firstly, the removal of virtually every established Kikuyu leader ended for the time being the political predominance of the tribe, giving leaders from other tribes the chance to emerge as national figures when the Administration permitted; at the same time, a 'new generation' of Kikuyu political leaders was brought into being, thus ending the remarkable continuity of Kikuyu political leadership over the previous 20 years or more. Secondly, the Emergency was the cause of shattering social and economic change among the Kikuyu: with the herding of the entire population into villages and the subsequent land consolidation programme, the complex processes of social stratification which had been underway for some time were immeasurably accelerated, and assisted too by the removal of many of the remaining restrictions on Africans growing cash crops such as coffee. Thirdly, this ongoing process, coupled with the division of the Kikuyu in the mind of government but also to some degree in reality into 'loyalists' and 'Mau Mau sympathisers' provoked cleavages in Kikuyu society which are still relevant in contemporary Kenyan politics.

Land and Politics

The mainspring of these changes in Kikuyu country was land consolidation—the consolidation of fragmented holdings into single units, and their subsequent registration under freehold title. It is true that many of the events which vitally affected Kikuyu political and social developments predated the mass consolidation programme—the herding of the population into fortified and guarded 'Emergency villages', for example or the formation of loyalist Home Guard units to fight the forest fighters and root out their sympathisers in the villages,

[22] See for example G. F. Engholm, 'African Elections in Kenya', in *Five Elections in Africa*, eds. W. J. M. MacKenzie and K. E. Robinson (London, Oxford University Press, 1960); George Bennett, *Kenya: A Political History* (London, Oxford University Press, 1963); Bennett and Carl Rosberg, *The Kenyatta Election: Kenya 1960-61* (London, Oxford University Press, 1961); Oginga Odinga, *Not Yet Uhuru* (London, Heinemann, 1967); Tom Mboya, *Freedom and After* (London, Heinemann, 1963).

or Operation Anvil, whereby thousands of Kikuyu were rounded up in Nairobi and on Rift Valley farms and sent either to detention camps or back to the Reserve. But once consolidation got under way, these issues became inextricably bound up with the land reform, as did the issue of when to end the Emergency and release the remaining 'hard core' of detainees.

Consolidation of the Kikuyu lands and the introduction of some form of title had been discussed within the Administration for some years, in response to the changes in tenure which were taking place independent of Government action, but by the outbreak of the Emergency there was no clear policy in favour of land consolidation. The fighting, however, changed all that, and led to the rapid abandonment of the view that 'community' (i.e. *mbari*) controls on tenure should be retained or strengthened.

Initially, Government action on Kikuyu land during the Emergency did not involve consolidation but confiscation. In December 1953 the Forfeiture of Lands Act was passed, providing for the confiscation of land individually owned by 'terrorists', whether they were convicted and imprisoned or at large. Forfeiture conditions were later extended to cover *mbari* lands as well, and by 1956 3,510 people, including 868 from Murang'a, had had their land taken away and initially set aside under the Act for 'public purposes'—markets, schools, and the like.[23] Six months later, the War Council decided to enforce the villagization of the K.E.M. tribes (i.e. the Kikuyu, Embu and Meru, although the Meru scheme was later abandoned), and within 15 months 1,077,500 Kikuyu and Embu had been forced to move into 854 villages—a policy which drew its inspiration, if that is the word, from the fortified villages of the Malayan Emergency.

Both these schemes, forfeiture and villagization, were seen as part of the evolving policy of 'rewards and punishments' which the Administration was pursuing. The Kikuyu were to be shown that individual forest fighters were punished with the loss of their land, and the whole tribe for their transgression in supporting the 'terrorists'. In the early stages at least, the 'rewards' were meagre and negative—the absence of the most rigorous forms of repression in 'co-operative' villages. In pro-Mau Mau areas, villagers were subjected to stringent curfews, were not allowed to leave their villages to cultivate their *shambas* or take their produce to markets, and were subjected to security checks by colonial officials and Home Guard units, often assisted by the hooded informers of the detention camp circuit. Villagization also had the very obvious security advantage of cutting off the men of the forest from the 'passive wing' of their supporters, and villagers could be conveniently subjected to very intensive anti-Mau Mau propaganda. Soon

[23] Sorrenson, op. cit., p. 105.

after villagization was complete, however, the rewards for co-operation with the colonial government became more substantial. Home Guards and other trustworthy individuals were allowed to grow coffee and other cash crops, and were permitted to indulge in commerce and move more freely around the district than were their less malleable fellows.

Land consolidation, too, was originally put into operation in sections of Fort Hall and Nyeri as a 'carrot' proffered to selected loyal areas. The DC's of the two districts were quick to point out to their superiors the security advantages of consolidation. By November 1955 it was province-wide policy, although the issue of land titles was left in abeyance because of legal difficulties and internal administrative problems about the type of title to be issued. From its inception as official policy, the main justification of consolidation for officials was political. It was hoped that it would create a rural bourgeoisie 'too busy on their land to worry about political agitation', as the Special Commissioner for Central Province put it.[24]

> Thus land consolidation was to complete the work of the Emergency: to stabilize a conservative middle class, based on the loyalists; and, as confiscated land was to be thrown into the common land pool during consolidation, it was also to confirm the landlessness of the rebels.[25]

And, for this piece of social engineering to be successful, it was imperative to 'strike while the iron was hot'—a favourite official slogan at the time—while the Kikuyu were still reeling from the other measures imposed on them, and before too much pressure built up in Kenya and abroad for the ending of the Emergency and the release of the 'troublemakers' who might ruin the whole project. This sense of urgency, and the original political motivation of the scheme (to which had by now been added all sorts of 'agricultural' arguments, which were in themselves highly political) inevitably affected the way in which consolidation was implemented. In Kiambu District it worked relatively smoothly, where the influence of the forest fighters had all along been somewhat less marked, and where too the proximity of Nairobi's commercial opportunities had long ago led to substantial support for freehold title. But in Fort Hall and Nyeri there were complications, not the least of them political.

Fort Hall had been the most conservative district in regard to land tenure, and also the most fragmented, particularly in the thickly populated middle zone of the district. There had been less demand for title than in either Nyeri or Kiambu, and government efforts to get

---

[24] Quoted in Sorrenson at p. 117.
[25] Ibid., p. 118.

consolidation moving were met by passive but dogged resistance. A more powerful factor than social conservatism (a term which perhaps explains little in itself) was political opposition: Fort Hall was probably the most determinedly pro-Mau Mau district in the country, and the Administration's scarcely concealed pre-occupation with the political advantages of consolidation made opposition the more consistent. An assessment of the political composition of the district in 1954 ran as follows: 10% of the population actively involved in Mau Mau, 70% passive supporters of the movement, 10% actively against it (Home Guards, Tribal Police, and some government servants and mission adherents), and 10% passively anti-Mau Mau (employees of government or of Europeans).[26]

Due to this popular resistance and to administrative and technical inadequacies, by the end of 1957 only 98,000 acres of fragments had been measured in Fort Hall, compared to 200,000 in Kiambu and a similar acreage in Nyeri.[27] The annual report for the following year showed that the Fort Hall figure had been almost trebled, but the same document foreshadowed the problems ahead: three locations had had to be demarcated again because of hopeless inaccuracies. During 1959 and 1960, it became plain that land reform in Fort Hall had been a fiasco. Aerial surveys showed large discrepancies between the consolidation register and ground maps—discrepancies far larger than the 5% considered acceptable and accountable due to technical mistakes of minor proportions. Political pressure and government enquiries gradually revealed evidence of substantial corruption, of fictitious fragments of land being recorded, and of repeated contravention of the appeals procedure laid down in the Land Tenure Rules. No prosecutions were ever instituted, the government being content to dismiss those officials under the strongest suspicion of corruption and ineptitude. The new consolidation ordered by government started in the latter half of 1960, but this time it proceeded more slowly—with most of the detainees returned, and with the re-emergence of legal nationalist politics, 'it was no longer possible to push people around by the actual or threatened use of a detention order'.[28]

In addition, the loyalists who had dominated the adjudication committees were being pushed off in some parts of the district by ex-detainees, who were far more likely to question decisions and procedures and to settle old scores with the committee members who had discriminated against them. In Fort Hall at any rate, the return of

---

[26] The material on land consolidation in Fort Hall is drawn mainly from Sorrenson, Chapter X, supplemented by my own information.
[27] Fort Hall District Annual Report, 1957; Central Province Annual Report 1957.
[28] Sorrenson, op. cit., p. 179.

the vast majority of the detainees in the years 1958 to 1961 was accompanied by greater resistance to consolidation, and the formation of the anti-consolidation secret society, Kiama kia Muingi (literally Council of the Many—i.e. the masses). Indeed, in at least one location of the district consolidation was not completed until 1968 because of popular resistance.[29]

Sorrenson's study clearly establishes one crucial point: that those who made the most substantial gains from consolidation were 'the rich, the powerful and the loyal'.[30] In practice, these three groups were one.

The active loyalists were government servants such as chiefs, and those Kikuyu who by commercial activity or the acquisition of non-*mbari* land had acquired an interest in the system which the forest fighters threatened. Sorrenson's assertion that the active loyalists were from the 'landed and wealthy classes' is supported, for example, by an analysis of the Githunguri Home Guard (Kiambu) by the District Officer in charge of it. Eighty-four per cent of the Unit's leadership was classified as 'rich or very rich', and of the rank and file numbering 609 men, just over 50% fell into the same category, with a further 23% listed as 'above average in wealth'. Sorrenson comments: 'There is no reason to suppose that this generalization was not also true of Fort Hall and Nyeri'.[31] At the other end of the scale, the core of the forest fighters, or at least of that majority which came from the rural areas, consisted of those who had little or no land—dispossessed *ahoi*, repatriated migrant labourers, and former holders of **githaka** plots which had been taken over by more fortunate or more astute lineage members. Allied to them, it appears, were the bulk of the small peasants, who had been subject to increasing pressure in the years preceding the Emergency from the breakdown of the communal system and population increase. It was this group which lost most during consolidation.

Initially, of course, smallholders in prison or in the forest were liable to have their lands confiscated under the Forfeiture Act, but the effect of this was comparatively limited. Far more important was the procedure adopted at a later stage, after consolidation had been completed in a given area, for lodging appeals against the decisions of consolidation officers and committees. It was fairly elaborate, allowing

---

[29] Sorrenson is wrong in stating at p. 181 that consolidation was complete in Fort Hall at the time of writing. Aside from two locations in Kandara Division where completion has been prevented by the opposition of the local population, a further section in the north-east of the district was not completed until 1968 because it was a low-priority area, dry and sparsely populated.
[30] Sorrenson, op. cit., p. 212.
[31] Ibid., p. 107-8.

for 30-day periods for appeal at three stages. On the face of it, it was fair enough, especially since those in detention were to be informed of consolidation proceedings. There can be little doubt, however, that the Land Tenure Rules did not operate that fairly. Firstly, the better educated, wealthy landowners were at an advantage over illiterate small peasants. Secondly, there is considerable evidence that detainees were not invariably informed of consolidation in their home areas, although some Administration officials behaved scrupulously in this regard.[32] There were, however, two important factors which made it almost impossible for administrators to deal fairly with detainees and with those who had grievances about consolidation. Consolidation was, after all, intended among other things to deprive the politically suspect of their land as a punishment for rebellion, and it requires considerable credulity to imagine that most district officers considered detainees to be innocent of 'terrorism' because the colonial authorities had not troubled to go through the formality of convicting them in court. Secondly, to a man consolidation officials were determined that the land reform should be irrevocable. And both the Suspension of Suits Acts and the later Registration Act effectively excluded appeals to the courts over consolidation matters. But even before that time, under the exigencies of political urgency, officials were 'damping down' appeals as best they could.

The precise socio-economic significance of the Emergency will doubtless continue to be the subject of argument for some time to come: some data on its consequences will in fact be presented and discussed in the concluding chapter of this book. There can, however, be little dispute over some of the major consequences which are most relevant to this study. Even if, as has sometimes been argued, the Emergency did not radically alter the distribution of land ownership in the Kikuyu Reserve, what it indubitably *did* was to consolidate and stabilize the position of the pre-Emergency powerholders in Kikuyu society. The importance of this fact is difficult to overestimate: the course of rural politics in the Kikuyu areas since the end of the Emergency demonstrates how versatile and successful the peasant leadership group has been (as has the urban political and business elite it supports) in fending off challenges and extending its control over the peasant society.

In the late Forties and early Fifties, the Kikuyu Reserve was approaching a state of political (and quite probably economic) crisis

---

[32] See for example the following Parliamentary Reports: August 1st, 1963, cols. 1629-45; March 11th, 1964, cols. 704-28; June 23rd, 1964, cols. 457-58; August 5th, 1964, cols. 1336-38; and especially November 5th, 1965, cols. 139-90.

which reflected the intolerable pressure of colonial incorporation not only as a *political* fact, but as an arrangement for extracting an *economic* surplus from the peasantry as well—mainly in the forms of taxes and of labour for the settlers—in conditions of rapid population growth and extreme land pressure. If the peasant militancy which this exploitation provoked posed a threat to the colonial administration, it clearly also placed at risk the position of those who depended on colonialism directly for their livelihood (chiefs, headmen and the like), or for the protection of their possessions (those who had effectively 'commercialized' *githaka* land), or for maintaining access to desirable roles within the system (sections of the intelligentsia—some teachers and mission school graduates, for example).

The Emergency ensured that the nationalist leadership (in both its militant and more conservative manifestations) was physically removed from the scene, the peasantry suppressed by military repression of an exceptionally violent and thorough kind, and the way opened for rural elites to consolidate their economic and social primacy while the 'new generation' of politicians moved in after 1955 to establish political bases among the unrepresented Kikuyu. Indeed it is likely that the 'new men' later performed an essential brokerage role between the rural landowners and colonial servants who had incurred nationalist hostility because of their Home Guard role, and the leadership which emerged from detention camps and prisons to assume prominent roles in the KANU organization.[33] The nationalist movement after the Emergency, as embodied in KANU, thus purported to represent even more diverse social forces than it had before 1952. To the ideologies of nationalism represented by, for example, James Gichuru on the one hand and Bildad Kaggia on the other, were added the ambiguous politics of new men such as Julius Kiano or Kariuki Njiiri. Through the rural KANU organizations these politicians led, the interests of those who had taken no part in the movement—indeed had bitterly opposed it—could be adequately expressed and protected, even though diffused through the rhetoric of nationalist politics.

---

[33] One example is perhaps Kariuki Njiiri, one of the two Murang'a MPs elected in 1961. Later an Assistant Minister, until his electoral defeat in 1969, he is the U.S.-educated son of ex-senior chief Njiiri Karanja, former leader of the Fort Hall Home Guard.

Chapter II

THE POLITICS OF INDEPENDENCE

The KANU government which took power in mid-1963 and led Kenya to independence at the end of the year represented, as was implied in the previous chapter, the fusion of a number of disparate social and political groups. What gave it its 'national' character was the breadth of the ethnic support which gathered round the central Kikuyu-Luo coalition; at the same time, the party encompassed a quite marked ideological dichotomy reaching up into the highest echelons of the leadership.[1] And, as far as the Kikuyu at least were concerned, these latter political differences reflected, to some extent, the social and economic tensions of the countryside.

In terms of its social and political composition, therefore, KANU had very little in common with the Kikuyu revolutionary movement whose mantle it claimed to inherit, and a number of whose leading personnel were now prominent KANU figures. It was far more akin to nationalist movements elsewhere in Africa, in its recruitment of the major ethnic and educational elites and in its adaptation to the style and the rules of terminal colonial politics: after a period of uncertainty in which it seemed possible that KADU, with its settler and colonialist allies and minority tribal support, might attain state power (because of KANU's internal problems as much as anything) it became clear that KANU, as the majority party, would win through in the inheritance situation.

The Majimbo constitution which was finally produced before independence was, in a sense, the price that KANU had to pay for expediting the elections and self-government. The time between Kenyatta's release in August 1961 and the 1963 elections had been one in which KANU had experienced great difficulty—in spite of *Mzee's* long-awaited leadership—in keeping factional conflict under control in

---

[1] See 'The Political Legacy' in C. J. Gertzel's *The Politics of Independent Kenya* (London, Heinemann, 1970).

the face of determined KADU efforts, assisted by the settlers, to ensure that real power would lie in the regions, and not in Nairobi. Kenyatta's release had not led to a decline in intra-party disputes: indeed, with the simultaneous release of Paul Ngei, Kaggia and some of the other nationalist 'hard-liners', Odinga gained much-needed allies in his struggle with Tom Mboya, Gichuru and Dr Julius Kiano, the leaders of the opposing faction, while in the Kikuyu rural areas KANU's political control was to some extent threatened by a recurrence of oathing and the resurrection of the revolutionary Land Freedom Army. The firm prospect of pre-independence elections, after the frustrating year of coalition government of KANU and KADU, may well have prevented KANU from falling apart, even though the nomination of parliamentary candidates provoked bitter quarrels at the local level.[2]

Although local issues were for the most part predominant in these nomination battles, in some areas they reflected the differences within the national KANU organization: in Central Nyanza, for example, Odinga was unsuccessfully opposed by Walter Odede, Tom Mboya's father-in-law, and in Kandara, Kiano organized a campaign to prevent Odinga's ally, Kaggia, from being nominated.[3] Paul Ngei was driven to form the African People's Party in Ukambani (which beat KANU in the Kamba areas) after a challenge to his leadership of the tribe.

The independence constitution gave substantial powers to the Regional Assemblies, the most important of which were control over the Administration and over land settlement, and the power to raise revenue by a Graduated Personal Tax. Odinga relates, however, how his Home Affairs Ministry circumscribed the regions' administrative control by refusing to allow District Commissioners, District Officers and chiefs to be employed by the regions, but 'seconded' them to their new employers, thus fulfilling the letter of the constitution while retaining considerable influence over the officials.[4] And the central government remained the major source of regional revenues, since it had been accepted that it would take the regional governments some time to collect enough GPT to operate their finances independently. But in any case, Majimbo (regionalism) was clearly seen to be the temporary price which KANU had paid for independence—within weeks of the pre-independence talks, government leaders were already declaring that 'Majimbo is dead'. It was of course finally killed off by the republican constitution brought into effect a year after independence.

The most important part of the independence package accepted by

[2] For an account of the 1963 election, see Clyde Sanger and John Nottingham, 'The Kenya General Election of 1963', *Journal of Modern African Studies,* No. 2, 1964.
[3] See Chapter Three below for a detailed account of Kiano's campaign.
[4] Odinga, op. cit., p. 243.

KANU was the agreement involving British Government loans for buying out white settlers, and for compensation and pensions for retiring expatriate civil servants. Under the independence settlement, no less than half of the total £50m. 'aid' package came under these heads.[5] KANU found itself, in short, agreeing to pay for and protect the white settlers and the civil servants who had run the colony largely for the benefit of the Europeans, as the price for control of the Kenyan state. As Gary Wasserman has pointed out: 'Land was the proof of the pudding whereby the new government could establish its credentials as a trustworthy client to the international financial and political network in which it sought membership.'[6] This agreement was especially repugnant, naturally, to the militant nationalists, who pointed out that the white settlers had acquired their land at the expense of the African people, and that the officials had likewise been unwelcome; it was therefore unreasonable to expect the poor and newly-independent state to foot the bill for the departure of these uninvited guests.

Clearly, there were a number of reasons for the relatively quiescent acceptance by the nationalist leadership of British terms. First and foremost was the fact that the nationalists wanted independence and full political control as quickly as possible; all other considerations were strictly secondary. But, as the quotation from Wasserman's study of the settler issue implies, to the extent that the terms involved issues of the 'confidence' of investors and aid agencies in the new government's willingness to meet its (colonially-defined) commitments, the gap between Britain and the incoming government, or at least important sections of it, was not very great. Partly, this was a matter of general agreement on priorities in key areas—such as land consolidation as well as settlement—where the interests of the settlers, their British protectors and the incoming elite more or less coincided. But more importantly the new elite could have no full idea of the nature of the commitments it was undertaking—to financial orthodoxy, to smallholder agriculture, to protection of large farms and estates—and the degree to which, in the years following independence, this commitment to capitalist policies circumscribed what the government could do without risking retaliation, both from 'donors' and from investors.

Opposition to land and settlement policies remained confined, for the most part, to the handful of Kikuyu radicals in Parliament, led by Bildad Kaggia, whose attacks on the government's policies finally led to his departure to the back benches in June 1964.[7] On another level, however, the conflict about goals and policies manifested itself in

[5] *British Aid 2: Government Finance* (London, Overseas Development Institute, 1964), p. 61.
[6] Wasserman, op. cit.
[7] See Chapter Three below.

factional struggles within the KANU parliamentary party, and in key areas of the countryside as well. There was of course nothing new about factionalism in KANU; what was clearly significant in the period from 1963 to 1966, however, was that factional groups chose to define themselves, or at least to defend themselves, in ideological terms.

Factions and Ideologies

A particular focus of this conflict in the first half of 1964 was the extremely active Backbenchers' Group, with Kaggia as its chairman, which initiated a number of resolutions and motions in Parliament critical of government policies, and which issued statements to the press which at times severely embarrassed the Cabinet—for example, the joint statement by KANU and TANU (Tanzania) backbenchers accusing the leadership of dragging its feet over East African Federation. The dominant members of the group at this time were undoubtedly the 'Odinga group', although both Odinga and Oneko, as members of the Cabinet, opposed the backbenchers on several occasions.

The membership of this radical faction, or at least of its most prominent membership, was virtually identical to the members who broke with KANU in April 1966. Odinga and Oneko were the only members in the Cabinet, but were supported by Kaggia and Tom Okelo-Odongo, both parliamentary secretaries, J. D. Kali, the Chief Whip, and a number of—mostly—Luo and Gusli—backbenchers, assisted by Pio Pinto, a Goan MP who was subsequently assassinated.

It seems as if the opponents of Odinga were not able to muster much support among the backbenchers against him until after the dissolution of KADU in November 1964, when the 'conservatives' were augmented by a good number of KADU members. Odinga's Cabinet opponents were led by Mboya and Gichuru, his old enemies, supported by Kiano, Njoroge Mungai, and the Attorney General, Charles Njonjo. The Mboya group seems to have operated against Odinga almost entirely within Cabinet circles, with little or no attempt being made to undermine his position in the House or in the country at this stage. Thus the signs of opposition which Odinga detected during 1964—Cabinet meetings being 'faced with decisions that had been taken outside by a group of the Ministers acting as a caucus',[8] signs comparatively unimportant in themselves, that he was falling out of Kenyatta's favour, while Mboya and Njonjo, pre-eminently—were gaining.

Ngala's announcement that KADU was being disbanded and its members joining KANU was greeted by KANU MPs as a suitable gesture of national unity on the eve of the first anniversary of *uhuru* and the imminent assumption of republican status under a unitary constitution.

[8] Odinga, op. cit., p. 276.

Perhaps more important, however, was the effect that the merger had on both the structure and ideology of the governing elite. It was not merely that the KADU MPs quickly forged links with the Mboya/Njonjo faction (if, indeed, these did not already exist) which, as the campaign against Odinga gathered force during 1965, eroded or scared off his support among KANU MPs and prepared the ground for the expertly-handled denouement of 1966.

Organization of the campaign against the Odinga faction must have started very soon after Odinga became Vice-President: by April 1965, Odinga's opponents felt strong enough to acknowledge publicly the existence of a group, composed mainly of backbenchers, who were known as the Corner Bar Group after the Nairobi restaurant in which they met. At its inaugural meeting, the group laid plans for attacking the Lumumba Institute, the Soviet-financed KANU party school with which Odinga and Kaggia were closely involved, for combating the 'communists' in Parliament, and for 'curbing Jaramogi's efforts'.[9]

It became plain to MPs during 1965 that Parliamentary activities against Odinga and his associates had at least the tacit support of the President. Support for motions by pro-Odinga MPs fell off sharply, and the informal role of backbenchers such as Ngala took on a new importance. Thus Ngala's motion in July 1965, proposing a new Sessional Committee which omitted the names of Oneko and Okelo-Odongo, was carried in spite of opposition by a Government spokesman, after Ngala had asserted that he had consulted the President.[10]

The anti-Odinga strategy, broadly, involved the isolation of the hard core of his supporters within Parliament and public attacks, not so much on Odinga himself—who was after all the Vice-President—as on Kaggia and Oneko, while attempts were made to undermine the constituency bases on Odinga supporters. Thus there were KANU elections resulting in new officers being installed in Murang'a, Homa Bay, Kitui and South Nyanza—all of them areas with pro-Odinga MPs. Mboya's role as Secretary-General of the party was central in this, since it was his responsibility to approve of the elections as having been properly conducted. At the same time, Odinga himself was gradually stripped of all but ceremonial functions, and his role within the Government and as leader of government business in Parliament became increasingly empty.

[9] Odinga reproduces the minutes of this meeting at pp. 289-91. The authenticity of the document seems beyond doubt: the Assistant Home Affairs Minister, Jeremiah Nyagah, whom the document identifies as having been present, quoted from it with approval in Parliament. See Parliamentary Reports, April 30th, 1965, cols. 1731-2. 'Jaramogi' is the title, meaning son of Ramogi, mythical father of the Luo people, commonly accorded Odinga.

[10] Parliamentary Reports, July 28th, 1965, cols. 1493-1524. The spokesman was Dr F. L. M. Waiyaki, who had some associations with the Odinga faction.

The Limuru Schism

The culmination of the campaign was the KANU Reorganization Conference, held at Limuru in March 1966. The choice of the conference as the technique for finally getting rid of Odinga and his supporters is an interesting one: KANU was sorely in need of overhaul, and was some £50,000 in debt; headquarters rent was unpaid, and no national officials had been elected since 1960. It was also true, however, that neither Mboya nor any other major political figure had made any visible effort to do much about party reorganization previously. The decision to hold the conference, then, seems to have been made on the grounds that nothing further could be done against Odinga in Parliament and government, and that the conference would demonstrate his lack of support in the party and at the same time prepare KANU, in its reorganized form, for political battle.

The primary weakness of the Odinga faction, of course, was that it was clearly a minority, not only in Parliament but among the delegates who arrived for the three-day conference. A further weakness, however, lay in Odinga's strategy: during the pre-conference skirmishes in Parliament and later at the conference itself his supporters relied on references to the KANU constitution and 'national unity' in attempting to counter hostile actions. This constitutionalism, even discounting the benefit of hindsight, seems to have been a gross political error in a party which had not held elections for almost six years when the constitution stipulated that they should be biennial; where the district branches had long since lost any semblance of mass organization and orderly procedure, if they had ever possessed it; and where the secretary-general, responsible for the general organization of the conference and in particular for the accreditation of delegates, was not only himself holding office unconstitutionally, but was the moving spirit of the opposing faction.

Thus Bildad Kaggia was elected KANU Vice-President for Central Province by provincial delegates on the second day of the conference, beating James Gichuru, Mboya's ally, by 20 votes to 12. On the following day, however, the result was reversed by the simple expedient of withdrawing the accreditation of some delegates, substituting others favourable to Gichuru, and holding another election, which predictably resulted in victory for Gichuru.[11]

Odinga's efforts were defeated—the new constitution was adopted by the party, his attempts to unseat Mboya as secretary-general failed, and he was not even elected Vice-President for Nyanza Province, where previously he had been national vice-president of the party. And

---

[11] *East African Standard* March 14th, 1966; interview with Bildad Kaggia, May 25th, 1967.

Kenyatta publicly announced his approval of the decisions on the final day, completing Odinga's humiliation and making his position in both party and government untenable. Odinga left the conference, and shortly afterwards accepted the invitation by a group of erstwhile KANU supporters to lead a new party, called in due course the Kenya People's Union.

The 'Little General Elections' which followed resulted in a similarly decisive defeat for Odinga's supporters, although as expected Odinga and his leading supporters retained the allegiance of the Luo community without difficulty, and gathered two seats in neighbouring Western Province and one Senate seat in Ukambani—a total of nine out of the 29 contested. In the Kikuyu areas, however, where the two seats of Kandara and Gichugu were at stake, the KPU vote was very small indeed.

In the areas where its mass support lay, the KPU was drawing at least as much on the ethnic solidarity of the Luos as on specific commitment to its radical policies; conversely, each vote for the party in the Kikuyu constituencies represented a firm rejection of what KANU was seen to stand for—in the face of very considerable intimidation as well as overwhelming ethnic pressure. Although the poll results, particularly in Kandara, are open to question on grounds of undoubted violence against KPU supporters and subsequent allegations of ballot-rigging, Lionel Cliffe's study of the Kikuyu contests suggests that KANU retained the loyalty of the majority of the voters not simply because of ethnic feeling or Kenyatta's pre-eminence, important though these factors were. The effect of the challenge posed by the KPU was to unite the bulk of the smallholders behind the relatively wealthy in defence of newly-won security and perceived economic opportunities. The KPU drew support only from a 'hard core' of embittered landless people, many of them former forest fighters and ex-detainees who had not managed to reap any fruits from independence.[12]

The formation of KPU, and the limited support which it gathered outside the Luo areas, was thus symptomatic not only of the internal personal conflicts within KANU, but of evolving patterns of social stratification in Kenya. This process was perhaps nowhere as far advanced as it was in Kikuyu country, and in this latter area the radical opposition had gained least support. But this is not as contradictory as it might appear: aside from the tremendous ethnic and governmental pressure on wavering Kikuyu to vote for the ruling party, their

[12] I am grateful to Lionel Cliffe for a sight of his study; it was to have formed part of a now abandoned study of the election, and has not to my knowledge been published elsewhere. Gertzel, op. cit., has two chapters on the election, a general account and a case study (with John Okumu) of the contests in Central Nyanza.

perception of relative deprivation was dulled, and that of politically conscious tribes such as the Luo correspondingly heightened, by the conviction that the Kikuyu areas benefited more from government expenditure and assistance than did other parts of the country.[13] This externalizing of potential political conflict within Kikuyu society was perhaps not decisive in the elections, but it was a factor of growing importance in enabling the KANU government to retain control over the Kikuyu countryside in the ensuing years.[14]

The importance of KPU lay in its challenge to the assumptions governing KANU's approach to economic development. Where KANU's pre-occupation with such issues as Africanization of trade and of managerial positions within the commercial sector have reflected the aspirations and priorities of Kenya's nascent commercial and professional elite, the oft-repeated condemnation of those who wanted 'free things' (i.e. KPU supporters) could likewise be seen as a reference to a middle-class ethic of thrift and hard work. As David Koff suggested, KANU's appeal was to those Kenyans who sought to exploit to the full the existing economic structure—to get jobs in private industries and commercial enterprises, to expand production on their individual lands—rather than to take the uncertain and possibly dangerous step of altering the economic structure by nationalizing industry and redistributing land.[15]

Extension of Control

Precisely because of KPU's attempt to challenge KANU by appealing to the poor *mwananchi* of all tribes (while naturally maintaining its ethnic support among the Luo), the government became increasingly concerned with suppression of the KPU and with firmer control over political life.

In many respects, there was little that was new in this process: the Administration, for example, had by 1966 already won back most of the powers it had lost with Majimbo. What became apparent in the years following the Limuru conference, however, was the importance of the Administration's specifically *political* role, in countering the threat from KPU. Thus the long-standing power of the Administration to licence public meetings was used from its formation to its 1969 proscription, to prevent KPU public meetings. And it was the Administration which ensured that returning officers in August 1968

---

[13] Parliamentary debates, especially during 1965 and 1966, abound with MPs' criticisms of Kikuyu 'dominance' and special privileges.
[14] See G. B. Lamb, 'The Political Crisis in Kenya', *The World Today*, London, December 1969.
[15] *East Africa Journal*, August 1966.

disqualified every KPU local government candidate from standing in the forthcoming elections, with the result that all KANU candidates were returned unopposed.

The KANU leadership's strategy, in this and other actions, seemed to incorporate three main aims. Firstly, state power would be used to suppress the opposition, albeit under a cloak of legalism. Secondly, the bureaucracy could also be employed as a crutch, as it were, for the ailing KANU organization, especially at district level. Thus, for instance, the power of chiefs (under the Chiefs Authority Act 1967) to compel attendance at their meetings on pain of imprisonment was frequently used to ensure a full turn-out for KANU functions; other administrative services were also frequently provided. At the same time, however, the bureaucracy could also be used to control conflict within KANU itself, and in ensuring the effectiveness of the centre's powers of sanction and patronage over the party's district branches. The requirement that candidates for national and local elections should be approved by a registered political party, for instance, was immediately seen by MPs as conferring on the Cabinet considerable power over local party affairs, and also as increasing the power of the officials, from the Registrar of Societies downwards, who would be responsible for enforcement.

But perhaps even more significant than these specifically political duties which accrued to the bureaucracy after 1966 was the steady transfer of control of critical local resources out of local hands (i.e. out of the hands of local politicians) into the keeping of the bureaucracy. Before, politicians had competed in and at times exercised control over land settlement boards (which chose settlers for plots on settlement schemes), district agricultural committees, community development committees, and boards which allocated loans to small traders. In all these cases, officials progressively assumed chairmanship and, in practice, control. Ultimately, of course, even local government was deprived of its major responsibilities and sources of patronage (in January 1970, for roads, primary education and health services) in the centralization of power—and also of its major source of revenue, the Graduated Personal Tax.

This combination of closer control and selective distribution of government resources, manipulation of the law and intimidation, culminated in 1969 in a renewal of specifically Kikuyu nationalism through oathing, and in the outright suppression of the opposition. While this was clearly a political development of major importance, it had little effect on the basis of the KANU government's power, and in that sense the Kenyan government has remained as dependent as ever on its peasant base. The continued commitment of the politically important sections of the peasantry to the government-approved disposition of power and resources is the condition of KANU's predominance: the really critical questions about Kenyan politics therefore involve the internal dynamics of peasant society in conditions of rapid socio-economic change, and the flexibility of the elite in identifying, manipulating and controlling new trends in the countryside. These are wide issues, some of which will be discussed fully in the conclusion, in the light of the Murang'a evidence. The four chapters which now follow seek to lay the basis for that discussion, by describing the evolution and decline in Murang'a of political conflict based on social class, and by analysing how that conflict permeated other district institutions concerned, in a broad sense, with 'rural development'. The course of politics in this single rural district, it will be contended, offers important insights into the national political process, and into the nature and direction of Kenyan economic development.

Chapter III

POLITICAL CONFLICT IN MURANG'A

The KANU branch in Murang'a in the period 1963 to 1967 contained many of the conflicts and tensions characteristic of the party at the national level—endemic factional conflict in which geographical interest, ideology and political generation as well as personal ambition played important roles, organizational weaknesses which were both a cause and a product of these conflicts—as well as those which were particular to Murang'a, and which sprang from specific local issues. The distinction, however, is somewhat unreal: conflicts among Murang'a KANU notables about land policy, about co-operatives or about community development tended to become intertwined with wide issues concerning development strategy and the composition and ideology of the national government. This was, of course, in part because the issues which concerned politicians in Murang'a were those which were important to the country as a whole; more directly, however, Murang'a politicians could and did call on political resources outside the district to assist them in the pursuit of local goals. Further, the process of political competition and schism in the district also reflected changes in the structure of Kikuyu society, and adjustments on the part of political actors to cope with these changes.

The purpose of this chapter, then, is to trace the development of factional politics in Murang'a, and to give an idea of the way in which the organization of political conflict affected development programmes in the district. Later chapters will examine some of these effects in more detail.

The Factions Form

The existence of opposing groups within the district branch, each with an identifiable leadership and core of followers, was not apparent until the latter part of 1962, and the start of serious competition for the 1963 elections. The most prominent KANU figure in the district was Dr

Julius Gikonyo Kiano, Member of the Legislative Council for Murang'a from 1958 and one of the two Members for the district after the 1961 election, in many ways an archetypal member of the 'new generation' of political leaders who had arisen during the Emergency. His most eminent supporters in the district were for the most part men who had not been closely involved with the illegal nationalist movement: Kariuki Njiiri, the other Murang'a MP; Jesse Gachago, who had been involved in the Nairobi trade union movement, briefly holding the post of national organizer for Mboya's Kenya Federation of Labour; and ex-Senior Chief Ndung'u Kagori, a former Kandara Home Guard leader. Kiano had not succeeded in attracting the bulk of the released detainees to his side, although a few—notably Taddeo Mwaura, the KANU branch chairman from its foundation in 1961, and his protege Mwangi Thabuni, both of them from Kandara—had responded to Kiano's claim to be the unifier of Mau Mau and Home Guard, and to his claim of pre-eminence in Murang'a politics.

Rapid African political advancement was partly responsible for the lack of overt conflict between ex-detainees and the 'new generation' leaders: internal differences were sublimated, for the time being, in the heady struggle for decolonization. In addition, however, the 'hard-core' detainees who returned to Murang'a in 1960 and 1961 lacked the leadership and political resources to challenge an established political machine, manned by politicians who had been able to use the detainees' absence to consolidate their support among the electorate and establish valuable contacts with the Administration.

The detainees were also deprived, for some time after his release in late 1961, of the leadership of the most influential militant, Bildad Kaggia, who had been a fellow-defendant of Jomo Kenyatta at the Kapenguria trial. Kaggia had been asked in February 1962 to go to Naivasha to mediate in a quarrel in the KANU leadership there, and had evidently seized the opportunity to consolidate for himself an 'official' base in the party.

> I was released in December, and after only one month or so there was some confusion in the Naivasha branch, and some delegations came from Naivasha to see me. They asked me to go and help sort out the branch. I declined, but they insisted, so I said to them that they could not expect me to go unless they were prepared to make me their sort of figurehead, their chairman, with authority.
>
> All they wanted, they said, was someone influential to go and sort out the affairs of the branch, which was getting out of control. So I agreed and took up the chairmanship.[1]

---

[1] Interview with Bildad Kaggia, May 25th, 1967.

Kaggia's astuteness in agreeing to become the arbitrator in this dispute provided the Murang'a ex-detainees with a leader who had considerable official status within KANU, even if his action left the Murang'a branch intact in Kiano's hands.KANU leaders in Murang'a originally assumed that Kaggia would contest a Parliamentary seat in Naivasha against KADU;[2] but Kaggia, certainly, felt that Naivasha was a convenient base from which to organize a campaign for nomination in Kandara, while remaining assured of the Naivasha candidacy should he fail in his home district.

> It was obvious to everyone that when the time of the election came I would choose Naivasha. But this was not my idea at all—but anyway I thought it was still too early to think where I would contest. I never regarded myself as a Murang'a leader—I've never been like that—so I was thinking that wherever I felt best, I would contest there, but I had never decided for Naivasha.[3]

Kiano and his supporters, with Kaggia out of the way, attempted to block any late decision by him to return by holding nomination contests in each division of the district[4], assuming that divisions would become constituencies although electoral boundaries had not yet been set. Each KANU divisional council held a nomination meeting of KANU members, from which the chosen name was sent to the district governing council for formal approval. In Kandara, the nomination meeting approved Kaggia's candidacy in October 1962 against that of Johnson Muigai, a local leader from the south of the division. Kaggia maintains that he did not campaign for the nomination, and that it was a spontaneous act by KANU stalwarts; it is clear, however, that his supporters had been given the sign they needed by Kaggia's refusal to decide finally for Naivasha, even if Kaggia himself did not plan the campaign. Kaggia's staunchest followers, the ex-detainees who had not (or not yet) managed to acquire land or jobs, had during 1962 formed a secret movement which acted as a pressure group among KANU members, and which was a revival in style and sometimes in name of the Kiama kia Muingi, the 'Council of the Masses' of the later Emergency years.

It was characteristic of Kandara, the 'worst' Murang'a division during the Emergency, that political conflict should take so sharp a form. Kaggia's stand was one which emphasized the revolutionary elements of African nationalism, demanding firm action against the former loyalists. Muigai, in echoing Kiano's plea to loyalists and forest fighters to forget

---

[2] Interview with Mwangi Thabuni, April 6th, 1967.
[3] Kaggia, May 25 1967.
[4] Mwangi Thabuni: 'Kaggia would know there was no room for him if he was foolish and wanted to fight KANU.' April 6th, 1967.

the past and work together, seems to have been widely interpreted as supporting the interests of the pro-colonial elements.

The party's district governing council, after an unsuccessful trip to Naivasha to persuade Kaggia not to accept the Kandara nomination, decided not to provoke a split by rescinding his nomination, but to involve Kenyatta's authority. Kaggia was summoned to Gatundu, and asked by Mzee to stand in Naivasha.

> But I told him, look here, Mzee, some people wanted you to stand in Murang'a, but you chose Gatundu instead. So I think it's also natural for me to choose my home district.[5]

When the list of KANU candidates was announced in February 1963, however, Kaggia's name had been replaced by Muigai's for the Kandara seat.[6] Kaggia, in a typically robust statement, accused Kenyatta of ignoring the wishes of Fort Hall people, and Kiano and Njiiri of holding secret meetings to undermine him.[7] Kaggia now made use of his Nairobi allies, with the result that Odinga was sent to Kandara by Kenyatta shortly before polling to preside over a new nomination contest, which Kaggia won. Kenyatta in this instance was acting in a way which was typical of his political style at the time: not so much arbitrating as responding to immediate factional pressures, but always ensuring that his decisions allowed sufficient flexibility to avoid schism. Thus he had initially acceded to pressure from the Kiano group, but then sent Kaggia's ally Odinga to settle the resulting dispute. After Kaggia's nomination victory, Kenyatta did not apparently attempt to intervene when Kiano's following, with the help of Mboya at party headquarters, gave active support to Muigai, who was standing as a KANU independent (the party HQ, in fact, did not give Kaggia any campaign assistance beyond the payment of his deposit). Kenyatta did, however, appoint Kaggia Parliamentary Secretary for Education after his victory over Muigai in the election by 25,193 votes to 8,420.[8]

Kaggia now started in earnest to build up his following in the Murang'a KANU branch, on the basis of his advocacy of the cause of the landless and the former forest fighters, and his opposition to chiefs and administrators who had served the British during the Emergency. All of the other Murang'a MPs—Kiano, Njiiri, Gachago and the district's Senator, Mwaura—were opposed to him, but he had some support among Regional Assembly and County Council members, as well as among locational leaders in Kandara and the other divisions.

[5] Kaggia May 25th, 1967.
[6] *East African Standard* February 14th, 1963.
[7] *Daily Nation* February 15th, 1963.
[8] *Daily Nation* May 28th, 1963.

Logically enough, the main focus of factional conflict was Kandara, where by mid-1963 the divisional party sub-branch was split into three by the supporters of Kaggia, Mwaura and Muigai. The existence of Muigai's faction reflected, in a sense, the tension in the alliance between Kiano and Mwaura: while Kiano had been Murang'a's most prominent politician in national terms since the late Fifties, Mwaura had concentrated on establishing a strong network of local influence in Kandara, and clearly had aspirations to district leadership. Muigai, on the other hand, owed such influence as he possessed in the district as a whole to Kiano's sponsorship—it was Kiano's influence, for example, which was decisive in gaining Muigai the chairmanship of the County Council in 1964. Within Kandara, Muigai's power seemed to be localized in locations 1 and 16, the southernmost locations bordering on the Chania River, where his home was. The population of the area, being somewhat isolated from both the Nairobi-Fort Hall road and the road to the District Officer's *boma,* were thought locally to be aggrieved by alleged neglect on the part of the Government.[9] Mwaura's following within the division was certainly more substantial and widespread.

Kaggia's supporters maintained their semi-clandestine organization in this period, and tried to develop a network of support in other areas while attempting openly to take over the Kandara sub-branch. The struggle intensified in the months immediately following independence, with the return from the Nyandarua Range of the last of the Murang'a forest fighters. Kaggia and Kiano were both present at rallies on January 15th, 1964, to receive guerillas who, it was reported, 'had held out so that they could talk with their leader, Field Marshal Mbaria Kaniu, who had been in restriction in Marsabit'.[10] The presence of both men provides an interesting contrast: Kaggia, as the spokesman of Mau Mau supporters, welcomed the men as heroes and potential supporters of his campaign; for Kiano, on the other hand, their return and the ritual surrender of their weapons were a public demonstration of his theme of Kikuyu and Kenyan reunification. In any case, he could not allow Kaggia to receive the guerillas alone, thereby legitimizing his claim to be their sole champion.

In the months following independence, the public expression of political conflict within KANU followed the familiar lines of the ex-forest fighters and deprived ex-detainees, led by Kaggia, ranging themselves against the Administration and the KANU hierarchy, the latter represented in Kandara by Mwaura. The ex-detainees formed a public body to advance their cause (apparently nameless, but widely

[9] District Officer Mandara, April 1967.
[10] *East African Standard* January 16th, 1964.

known as 'Mituikire'—the ragged ones), and made a series of demands for the return of confiscated land and the removal or punishment of chiefs who had served the British during the Emergency. Although the District Commissioner reported that it was disbanded late in the year after 66 members had been given settlement plots,[11] it seems that it, or a very similar body, remained active in Kandara politics as a pressure group within KANU.

In June 1964 Kaggia sustained a serious setback in national politics when he was dismissed from his Government post. His dismissal was not, on the face of it, the result of pressure on Kenyatta from members of the opposing Murang'a faction, as had been the case in the nomination battle. Kaggia, as chairman of the KANU Backbenchers' Group, had been partly responsible for a series of strongly-worded attacks on Government policy by the Group, notably over land settlement and the East African Federation issue. He was dismissed by Kenyatta when he refused to obey Kenyatta's warning to desist from public criticism.[12] Two facts might seem to argue to the contrary, however: Kenyatta criticized Kaggia in his warning letter for 'interfering with land consolidation in Fort Hall',[13] and Kaggia's successor as Parliamentary Secretary for Education was Jesse Gachago, Kiano's protege. Kaggia, certainly, was in no doubt that his dismissal stemmed from his radical stance on the issue of landlessness, and that it was therefore related to local political conflict.

Following his dismissal, Kaggia evidently felt the need to consolidate his local base in order to survive politically: he had been publicly cast from Kenyatta's favour, and his opponents in Murang'a were naturally using this fact to discredit him. In August, KANU branch elections were held at Fort Hall, and Kaggia was elected branch chairman. Of his lieutenants, James Beauttah became secretary, Mbaria Kaniu vice-chairman, and Kamau Mweru treasurer—as the *East African Standard* described it, a victory for the 'old guard'.[14] Beauttah had been deeply involved in Kikuyu nationalist politics since the heyday of the KCA, had been imprisoned for sedition in 1951 and restricted throughout the Emergency. Kamau Mweru, also a former detainee, had owned a small transport business before the Emergency, but his buses had been confiscated while he was in detention.

Ideologies in Conflict

The branch elections mark the beginning of a new phase in Murang'a politics. Up to that time factional conflict, although at times bitter and

[11] Murang'a District Annual Report 1964, p. 2.
[12] Parliamentary Report June 23rd, 1964, cols. 457-8.
[13] Ibid.
[14] *East African Standard* August 10th, 1964.

intense had been contained for the most part within areas where its influence on the administration of government was marginal. The KANU politicians were primarily concerned with control over their political organization—perhaps because the party was seen at that stage to control really important local resources (such as land settlement) through the Regional Assembly, and Government officers did not at that stage possess the political authority conferred on them after the abolition of Majimbo at the end of 1964. It is true that 'politics' had slowed down the land consolidation programme, but this had less to do with the specific anti-consolidation activities of Kaggia and his followers (which seem in any case to have been confined to ensuring that the re-consolidation ordered in 1960 was in fact done in all locations) than with the considerable and long-standing opposition to consolidation on the part of a substantial section of the Kandara population.

With the defeat of Kiano and his allies, however, the ideological aspects of political struggle assumed new importance. KANU was transformed to espouse radical political and social action on behalf of the dispossessed, and against those who had played a prominent role in its affairs in spite of their former anti-nationalist sympathies. The 'conservatives', deprived of their political base, sought to create or strengthen informal relationships with leaders in 'non-political' institutions such as coffee co-operatives, voluntary school committees and community development committees who were likewise out of sympathy with Kaggia and his militant supporters.

In a manner characteristic of KANU not only in Murang'a but elsewhere in Kenya as well, the branch election results were immediately challenged by the Kiano group, which alleged that the voters at the election were not proper local delegates—in other words that the meeting was 'packed'.[15] The organization of KANU provided ample evidence for such charges. The party in Murang'a had never existed as a mass party of card-holding members who paid regular dues, with elected local delegates who met annually to elect branch officials, despite the requirements to this effect of the KANU constitution. The office-holders in the branch had been holding office unconstitutionally, since there were no annual delegates' conferences between the establishment of the branch in 1960 and the election in 1964; in the local organizations, too, there had been few elections and little regularly-organized activity. Many local organizations were split (only a few of them, apparently, along Kiano/Kaggia lines). Perhaps most relevant of all, the active membership had declined sharply after independence, with many of the most prominent activists being

[15] Interview with Kamau Njoroge, May 15th, 1967.

absorbed into government or drifting away into commerce, and with the party's *raison d'être,* apart from its identification with Kenyatta and the government, apparently uncertain to the bulk of the population.

The factional groupings within the district, therefore, were operating in a context of generalized support for party and government, but with few organizational or constitutional norms to control the tactics of conflict. There was thus no question of authoritative accreditation of delegates to the 1964 election conference, or of effective appeals by the losers to an active and knowledgeable party membership.

Kiano's statement after the election asserted that the old officers remained the 'true KANU', and that Kaggia was not the chairman of the branch. There were thus two bodies, both claiming to be the party executive, from August 1964 to February 1965. There was no successful attempt by either group or by KANU headquarters to register either faction as the branch executive with the Registrar of Societies. The Kiano faction seems to have recognized, however, that Kaggia's claim could not easily be challenged; they concentrated on recruiting support outside KANU itself.

Sometime shortly after the elction, an organization known as Atiriri Bururi Union—Ndirira for short—was formed in Kandara, quite plainly to undermine Kaggia's home base.[16] The full name means 'Union of Patriots' (literally 'Supporters of the Country'); the abbreviation has been variously translated as 'one who stands with courage', 'patriot', and (with some irony, by Kaggia himself) as 'one who supports himself'. Prominent among its leaders were Mwaura, Ndungu Kagori, and Mwanga Thabuni. It was difficult to obtain details of Ndirira's support, but it is clear that much of it came from the personal followings of Mwaura and Kagori, many of whom were prominent in coffee co-operatives and school committees. Although there is no doubt that Ndirira was originally formed to oppose Kaggia, the influx of small shopkeepers and coffee farmers gave to its propaganda not only a 'class' character, but also a strongly anti-government flavour—particularly because of dissatisfaction among coffee farmers at the government's ban on new planting of coffee.[17]

In effect, Mwaura and his Kandara allies were attempting to create a political force which could rival the ex-detainee movement supporting Kaggia, which now had a status in KANU that Mwaura could not

---

[16] Some informants dated Ndirira from early 1964, but there is no clear evidence that it existed before the latter half of the year; it is probable that they associated the name with an earlier anti-detainee body whose existence was mentioned by several people, but whose leadership could not be identified.

[17] I am indebted to John Kamau and Kihara Waweru for much of the information on Ndirira.

effectively challenge. As an alternative to Kaggia's concentration on the plight of the landless and ex-detainees, Ndirira emphasized the *Harambee*[18] virtues of hard work, land ownership, social unity and self-help; the anti-government outbursts which characterized its first flurry of political activity in September and October 1964 were muted as its main purpose—opposition to Kaggia—was reasserted, and its leaders sought to invoke the support of the central government. In a manner similar to later anti-KPU propaganda, Kaggia was accused of wanting the government to hand out 'free things', of obstructing land consolidation and the planting of coffee, and of wishing to take away the land of all those who had neither fought in the forests nor been detained.

Both groups during this period held a number of public rallies at which the opposing side was ritually condemned, and the speakers endorsed as the true representatives of the masses. Simultaneous with these public manoeuvres, however, were changes in the allegiance of some formerly prominent members of Kaggia's side. Why they changed, or indeed exactly when, is not clear; some at least sensed that Kaggia's political future in Murang'a and in Nairobi was black, as Odinga and his allies were losing ground. The first public sign of this erosion of Kaggia's support was a petition, issued on February 11th, 1965, calling for the resignation of Kaggia as chairman of the Murang'a KANU branch. The signatories included Kiano, Mwaura, Njiiri, Gachago and Muigai, and also three of Kaggia's erstwhile supporters: Kiiru Mwangi, a provincial councillor, and two County Councillors, James Wainana and Micino Gichu.[19]

A significant point about the petition is that it acknowledged what the first five signatories had denied—that Kaggia was chairman of the party branch. It is possible that this admission was connected with a broader plan for the isolation of radical KANU leaders both in Murang'a and in other parts of the country. The petition attacked Kaggia for his 'statement at the weekend in Kisumu'[20] at the same rally at which Odinga was alleged to have equated Communism with food, a speech which provided much of the initial ammunition for the subsequent campaign against him. Kenyatta had paid a two-day visit to Murang'a two weeks before the petition, and had met district leaders—although not Kaggia and his fellows on the executive. Possibly one purpose of the visit was to decide on a strategy for eliminating Kaggia's influence. Moreover, the subsequent action against Kaggia had its counterparts elsewhere in Kenya.

[18] '*Harambee*', meaning 'pull together', was coined by President Kenyatta as a national slogan.
[19] *East African Standard* February 12th, 1965.
[20] Ibid.

Kenyatta paid a second visit to Murang'a on April 10th, and attacked Kaggia, who was on the platform with him, in a well-publicised speech in Kandara. Kaggia, Gichoya (MP for Gichugu in Kirinyaga, who joined KPU in 1966) and 'a certain Kiratu' had been advocating free things, he said. Turning to Kaggia, he berated him for remaining idle, while Kenyatta, Ngei and Fred Kubai had prosperous shambas, and Kungu Karumba owned a transport business (Ngei, Kubai and Karumba had also been on trial with Kenyatta at Kapenguria).[21]

This striking affirmation of bourgeois virtues, and the earlier anti-Communist petition, pointed to the increasing importance of ideology as the expression of cleavage in Murang'a as well as nationally. Although it could not of course be said that the political groupings in Murang'a changed their character at this single point in time, Kenyatta's speech demonstrated that the significant distinctions were those of social class and commitment or opposition to individual enterprise. Murang'a's conflicting political groups had been 'factions' in the sense that their ability to recruit support depended on allegiances to individual leaders, who recruited supporters on diverse principles;[22] over time, however, the ideological proclivities of the competing groups (and similar developments at the national level) had produced in Kandara particularly more exclusive recruitment of followers. In Murang'a during 1965, as in Nairobi, political alignments were more plainly drawn by the protagonists along lines of social class. The political themes of the actors involved were couched less in terms of organizational legitimacy and loyalty to *Mzee,* than in terms of the implications for particular strata of the population of supporting one or other group.

From the beginning, Kaggia had placed less reliance on the themes of national unity and *Harambee* than his opponents—indeed, he had concentrated on the divisions in Kikuyu society. He had, however, broadly limited his attacks on government policy to the unfair treatment of the ex-detainees, since he identified them as those Kikuyu in most urgent need of government resources.[23] After Kenyatta's attack, however, and the ensuing 'anti-Communist' campaign in Murang'a against Kaggia, he perceived that it was necessary for him to be seen as the spokesman for all the Kikuyu deprived groups, against those he felt were would-be exploiters and representatives of the wealthy.[24] Thus his reply to Kenyatta, to a student meeting at

[21] *Sunday Nation* April 11th, 1965.
[22] See Nicholas, op. cit. A fuller discussion of the nature of political groups in Murang'a is contained in the concluding chapter.
[23] See for example his speech in the Budget debate, June 23rd, 1964, cols. 450-8; also September 1st, 1964, cols. 1775-7.
[24] May 25th, 1967.

University College Nairobi, reaffirmed his commitment to socialism, and argued that planning should be based on popular discussion at the lowest level of KANU, instead of the government presenting the party with *faits accomplis*. His standing in Kandara had not been lowered by Kenyatta's attack, he claimed; the people knew that, far from supporting free hand-outs, he advocated that land should be given to all the poor and landless people, instead of to those who were already better-off, and that settlers should be given a three-year moratorium on repayments.[25] The reference to *faits accomplis* was a persistent argument of Kaggia's—that KANU's potential for social change and economic development had been dissipated because the leadership did not wish to submit to popular control through the party, and that Mboya in particular had been responsible for KANU ceasing to exist as a mass movement.

The Kiano faction, in the days following Kenyatta's visit, developed the theme that Kaggia was the enemy of all except a handful of forest fighters. Thus Kiano criticized Kaggia for 'eliminating the rich so that everybody could remain poor', and asked: 'Does he mean that private families may not have private houses or small farmers should be deprived of smallholdings? This is perhaps what he has in mind, but it will not work in Africa.'[26] This statement contains the essential elements of all the subsequent anti-Kaggia themes to be used in Murang'a during 1965, during the election in 1966, and afterwards: a frank appeal to the rich or would-be rich to protect themselves from being deprived of wealth or opportunity; arguing to the smallholders that their interests were identical to those of the wealthy, and were equally threatened by Kaggia; and an oblique suggestion that Kaggia's ideas were un-Kenyan, indeed un-African. In another press statement, Kiano demanded that Kaggia resign as KANU branch chairman, since he was a 'do-nothing politician' (an echo of Kenyatta's attack on Kaggia's 'idleness') who opposed self-help and Harambee schools.[27] A few days later, Kaggia was again charged with wishing to confiscate the property of smallholders.[28]

The Murang'a 'coup'

On May 2nd, a Kandara rally organized by Atiriri Bururi passed a vote of no confidence in Kaggia, and the following day a deputation, led by Mwaura, Thabuni and Ndung'u Kagori and accompanied by some 2,000

[25] *East African Standard* April 15th and 16th, 1965, and interview May 25th, 1967.
[26] *East African Standard* April 16th, 1965.
[27] *Daily Nation* April 19th, 1965.
[28] *East African Standard* April 23rd, 1965.

demonstrators, visited Kenyatta with a parcel alleged to contain 25,000 anti-Kaggia signatures. Kenyatta refused requests to sack Kaggia as MP and ban his meetings, but pointed out that no-one was compelled to go and listen to him.[29]

This was a public manifestation of a strategy, obviously already planned, to deprive of their influence, not only Kaggia, but other radical MPs as well. On May 15th, a meeting which had been advertised as a 'Senator's rally',[30] called by Mwaura, held elections for officials of the KANU branch. Kiano was elected chairman, Njiiri treasurer, Gachago secretary, and Mwaura branch executive officer, apparently a new post.[31] The same doubts and confusions about the propriety of delegates and about authorization to call the meeting, are not present here as they had been the year before. Kaggia, the acknowledged branch chairman, had not called the meeting, nor was he present, and less than a year had elapsed since the previous election in August 1964. Kaggia declared the election null and void, but the circumstances were very different this time. Within a month at least three KANU branch elections were held in other districts in which there were pro-Odinga MPs, all of which resulted in the election of executives hostile to the MPs—the one in South Nyanza was in fact also held on May 15th—and similar 'coups' were also staged in Mombasa, Machakos and Kisii. The coincidence of the elections, and Kaggia's account of what followed indicate the extent to which political conflict in Murang'a had become part of the ideological conflict within the national elite.

> When this was done, I went straight to the Registrar (of Societies) and I found that he had the names, he had not registered them, as he was still in doubt. I said that we are opposing this, because there was no election, and we can't accept any election that was done unconstitutionally. Because any election must be convened by me as chairman, and nobody else. Again it was not time for an election, because it was not even one year yet. So the Registrar told me he was waiting to hear from the KANU headquarters whether to register them or not. After two days I went again, and he didn't even talk to me, he just produced a letter from the Secretary-General, and he said, now I was not willing to register them, but now I've got instructions from KANU headquarters and these are the right officials, and therefore I'm going to register them. So I wrote a letter to the President, Vice-President and Secretary-General, complaining about this, but it was all

---

[29] Mwangi Thabuni April 6th, 1967; *Daily Nation* and *East African Standard* May 4th, 1965.
[30] Kamau Njoroge, May 15th, 1967; Kaggia May 25th, 1967.
[31] *Daily Nation* May 17th, 1965.

ignored. In a few days, the new officials were registered, and we were out. So that is how the coup was conducted.[32]

With the removal of Kaggia and his followers from KANU positions and the later banning of political meetings in Kandara, Kaggia was virtually confined to asking Parliamentary questions and moving critical motions; this disability, and the knowledge that the full weight of the Kikuyu national leadership was behind Kiano, accelerated the erosion of all but the most committed of his prominent supporters. Mbaria Kaniu accepted a settlement plot in Nyandarua; James Beauttah, while refusing to condemn Kaggia, played a less active political role; Kamau Mweru 'thought that politics in Murang'a had become so confused and so mixed up that it was better for him to go back to business.'[33] Kiiru Mwangi and Lawrence Karugo were given posts on the Fort Hall Trade Development Joint Board in July 1965, appointments under the control of Kiano, the then Minister of Commerce and Industry.

The board was abolished before they had participated in any of its meetings, however, and a new board established of which they were not made members. Kaggia's explanation of this affair was that Kiano had exercised his patronage to ensure the somewhat doubtful loyalty of the two men, who wielded some influence among traders in Fort Hall town, but had the decision reversed in November 1965 because they had not come up to his expectations. A later consideration—the abolition of the old board was announced in August, although the new board was only gazetted in November—was to provide a source of income, patronage and prestige as the new board's chairman for Kiano's ally Mwaura, who had been defeated in the August Senate elections by Robinson Mwangi Wanjagi (sometimes spelt Njagi or Njage), who was also appointed to membership of the board.[34]

The election of Wanjagi pointed to some of the structural complexities of what has been referred to above, for the sake of brevity, as the 'Kiano faction'. In fact the anti-Kaggia grouping revolved around a coalition of the followers of Kiano in Kangema, Kigumo and Kiharu divisions, and the Mwaura group in Kandara. Kiano's long pre-eminence in Murang'a politics has already been referred to: neither Gachago nor Njiiri possessed substantial independent followings, although Njiiri's local base was the stronger of the two latter because of his family connections and his longer career as an MP. Mwaura, on the other hand, had a committed following in Kandara and was not a protege of Kiano's in the same sense as the other two MPs. The coalition did not depend

[32] May 25th, 1967.
[33] Kaggia, June 24th, 1967.
[34] See Parliamentary Report January 26th, 1966, cols. 84-6; additional information from Kaggia, June 24th, 1967.

solely on unity in opposition to Kaggia as threat to Kiano's national ambitions and Mwaura's local base, but on at least a partial identity of wider interests and ideology. Kiano's support was, however, much more widely based than Mwaura's in geographical and social terms. Whereas the Mwaura faction in Kandara was seen in the district as the political vehicle of the Home Guards and the richer strata of Kandara society, Kiano retained the support in the other divisions of the majority of members of those social groups which in Kandara tended to support Kaggia. There were thus at least two potential sources of tension within the anti-Kaggia group: Mwaura's aspirations to reduce his dependence on Kiano, and the hostility of important sections of Kiano's following towards Mwaura and what he was seen as representing.

Wanjagi defeated Mwaura in the Senate elections by 16,998 votes to 14,803—the low poll of 26% being partly due to the relatively small amount of publicity accompanying the election, since only about fourteen Senators were standing for re-election, under the constitutional provisions requiring no more than one-third of the Senate seats to be vacant at any one time. It would have been interesting to know the distribution of voting within the district: there is a strong probability that the heaviest voting took place in Kandara, with the other three divisions showing much less interest. There were, however, legal obstacles to this information being given.

Wanjagi's victory was ascribed by the District Commissioner to the fact that he had 'both Kaggia support and a part of Mwaura support'[35]—that is, Mwaura was opposed by members of the Kiano faction outside Kandara, and was not conspicuously supported for re-election by Kiano himself. Wanjagi had been inactive in Murang'a politics since 1963, after a short period as an ex-detainee activist and supporter of Kaggia. He had been appointed to a post in the President's office at Gatundu in 1963, and it was not until early 1965 that he regained some prominence when the Kaggia-controlled KANU Governing Council nominated him as candidate for the Senate election. Although the commitment of Kiano himself to one or other candidate was not clear, it is quite probable that he welcomed Mwaura's defeat, since it reduced Mwaura's potential for threatening his leadership and made him more dependent on Kiano's patronage, while not substantially affecting his value as Kaggia's main opponent in Kandara. Certainly Kiano's attitude to Mwaura at the time of the Little General Election supports the supposition that Kiano was conscious of the need to allow Mwaura only a carefully circumscribed influence as a divisional leader. It is plain, at any rate, that a large section of Kiano's following outside Kandara supported Wanjagi, despite his having been Kaggia's

[35] Annual Report 1965, p. 1.

nominee: the District Commissioner's assertion that 'he was thought to be a good mediator between the two groups'[36] is relevant here. Wanjagi was not so uncomprisingly committed to the anti-Home Guard cause, and he had not been actively involved in the political conflicts of the recent past.

But Wanjagi does not seem to have played any active mediating role: he left for Europe shortly after his election, and did not return until December 1965. The election was followed, however, by a decline in overt factional conflict. Kaggia was aware of his growing isolation, both in Murang'a and in Nairobi. His ejection from the Murang'a KANU executive, Kenyatta's public censure, and the accusation that he was obstructing economic development had clearly had some effect, and the national campaign against the followers of Odinga was gathering momentum. The Administration, too, was more openly hostile, primarily because Kaggia had been publicly cast into the wilderness by the President.

In December, Kaggia began to participate with the other Murang'a MPs in the newly-formed District Development Advisory Committee, and attended a number of *barazas* called by civil servants in Kandara. He was also responsible, in February 1966, for getting a motion carried in Parliament with the support of all Murang'a MPs, calling for the rationalization of local authority and Administrative jurisdictions in the former Thika District. Kaggia asserted that these activities were a 'last effort' to unify the district and pull together[37]: he may also have been trying to challenge Kiano's leadership (and mollify the Administration) by becoming to some degree 'respectable'.

Kiano apparently felt this to be the case: in a press statement on February 11th, 1966, he announced that all Murang'a MPs had met at his initiative and agreed that political unity must be re-established. They had decided, he said, that no MPs would stand for office at the next KANU branch elections, and that KANU leaders would refuse to attend meetings at which other leaders were attacked.[38] The statement was obviously designed to create the impression that Kiano was once again taking the lead in settling political disputes and restoring unity to Murang'a. The other MPs denied, however, that such a meeting had ever taken place. In a reply also signed by five Provincial Councillors, Kiano's claim was denounced as 'inaccurate, premature, and prejudicial to unity'. All of the signatories had been discussing the problems of political unity in the Development Advisory Committee, they said, but no conclusive agreement had been reached.[39]

[36] Ibid., p. 2.
[37] Kaggia June 24th, 1967.
[38] See *East African Standard* February 12th, 1966.
[39] Ibid. February 24th, 1966.

Kaggia, who was responsible for this reply,[40] had thus succeeded, however temporarily, in publicly uniting the district's most prominent political leaders against Kiano, not on ideological grounds but by exploiting the tensions and discontents arising from Kiano's claim to primacy. It is, of course, impossible to judge whether he could have succeeded in any sustained anti-Kiano campaign; the pressures of national politics in early 1966 decided the Murang'a KANU leadership issue by impelling Kaggia to leave the party.

Kaggia's Defeat

Kaggia's decision to join Odinga and the other radicals after the Limuru conference reflected his realization that radical criticism would no longer be tolerated in KANU, either in Parliament or in the district branches.

> We did not want to split from KANU after the Limuru affair, but we looked at the branch coups that had taken place, and now a coup had taken place in the headquarters, and nobody was prepared to listen to our pleas.... We have done our best in all those years, we have persevered terrible treatment—myself, I had been very badly treated. First, I lost my job for voicing genuine grievances, and secondly I was assailed by the President himself here in Murang'a, and I was always taking these things very easily. But when it came to the Limuru coup, we decided that that was too much, and we couldn't go any further. We decided that now those people are determined to crush us, and to crush the proper public opinion, and we thought it was our duty now to take up a stand. There was no other way except to form a new party.[41]

Kaggia was, of course, compelled to stand for re-election in Kandara, where he was beaten by Mwaura by 20,230 votes to 2,170.[42]

The manner of Mwaura's selection as the KANU candidate reveals once again something of the structure of the anti-Kaggia group. Mwaura was, of course, extremely anxious to contest the seat, but met with considerable opposition from party headquarters and from other Murang'a leaders. Kiano, certainly, did not wish Mwaura to be nominated: at first, it appears, he wanted Johnson Muigai to be selected as Kaggia's opponent, and throughout the period preceding the election he worked actively to prevent Mwaura's selection. Kiano's motives may well have included his concern at Mwaura's ambitions; what concerned the Murang'a KANU leadership and the party headquarters even more,

[40] Kamau Njoroge May 15th, 1967.
[41] Kaggia May 25th, 1967.
[42] *Daily Nation* June 28th, 1966.

however, was the selection of a candidate sufficiently popular to match Kaggia's unquestionable influence. Plainly, KANU had several advantages in the election, not least its identification with Kenyatta and with the Government, and the active support of the Administration. But Kaggia also had some factors in his favour.

Following his resignation from KANU, he had had considerable success in persuading village and sub-locational leaders to maintain their support for him, even though several of the more prominent Kandara leaders had not left the ruling party with him. Kaggia had also been a very active and able MP, taking part in virtually every major debate, asking questions, compelling the Minister of Lands and Settlement to visit Kandara on several occasions to settle consolidation disputes, and taking the initiative over the sensitive issue of the district's boundaries. This activity was in marked contrast to Mwaura's record—the Senate had been relegated to the political sidelines by the Government soon after independence, and in any case Mwaura did not seem to have played a prominent role in its affairs.

Kiano's protege, Muigai, had been decisively defeated by Kaggia in 1963; moreover, there was considerable dissatisfaction in the division about his performance as chairman of the County Council. The same drawback, the geographically restricted nature of his support, applied in 1966 as in 1963 and, together with the other disadvantages, this effectively ruled out his candidature, despite Kiano's support.

Mwaura had announced that he would be the KANU candidate soon after the Government announced the election date, but the headquarters choice and that of the Murang'a executive was the Kandara Provincial Councillor Mburu Wanyoike. Wanyoike had been a supporter of Kaggia in 1963-64, but had apparently left the group shortly after Kaggia's election as KANU chairman. It was reasoned that Wanyoike would be able to attract more of Kaggia's supporters than their old enemy Mwaura, even if the latter had the authority of the President behind him. Mwaura was therefore summoned to Nairobi and asked to stand down, but refused to do so.

The formal nomination of the KANU candidate, as in the past, was the task of the Kandara sub-branch council, presided over in this instance by Kiano as branch chairman. As in 1964 and 1965, however, no-one could say with any certainty who the duly-elected delegates to the sub-branch council were—especially now that a substantial number of local leaders had remained loyal to Kaggia.

At the meeting, Mwaura's supporters secured him the nomination. (One informant asserted that the crucial votes for Mwaura came from men who still supported Kaggia although they had not formally renounced KANU membership, because they felt that Mwaura's nomination ensured Kaggia's victory.) Mwaura's nomination was immediately opposed by Kiano, who interceded with the party's national leadership to obtain a reversal. It was obvious, however, that in view of Mwaura's determination to stand, the candidate should be seen to be a local party nominee, if a potentially damaging split of the anti-Kaggia vote was to be prevented. Another Kandara nomination meeting was therefore held, presided over by Mboya as secretary-general of the party, and by James Gichuru, the Central Province vice-president. Once again, however, Mwaura was selected by the delegates, at a meeting at which Mboya was physically threatened by Mwaura's supporters for urging those present not to vote for their man, and Kiano had finally to assent.

From the outset, the Kandara election campaign was bitter and intense. Kaggia's rallies, apparently well-attended, were said to have been marked on occasion by the chanting of Mau Mau slogans and mass demands for the dismissal of Kandara administrators; the anti-Home Guard element in Kaggia's propaganda was even more to the fore than it had been in earlier political skirmishes. Mwaura's supporters, too, reiterated old themes—that Kaggia planned to collectivize or confiscate smallholders' lands, that no-one would be permitted to own a shop or business, and that only ex-forest fighters would qualify for favours.

The contest was also the most violent of the Little General Election. At least seven people were killed in the course of the campaign—Kaggia supplied the names of four of them whom he said, had been KPU supporters murdered by KANU youth wingers brought in from outside Central Province. A number of houses were burnt or demolished, and two KPU campaign cars were stoned by KANU supporters.

The climax of the campaign was an eve-of-poll rally addressed by Kenyatta at Ndungu Stadium, Kandara. The high point of Kenyatta's denunciation of Kaggia, according to press reports, was when he waved photographs of an '18-room mansion'[43] which he said was being built for Kaggia in Kandara, and asked the crowd where the money for this conspicuous consumption had come from. 'China', the crowd, reported as numbering 20,000, replied.[44]

Kaggia alleged that, apart from violence and intimidation directed against his supporters, the election was invalid because of the fraud which followed it. During the counting of votes, he said, he had caught two counters seeking to conceal KPU votes inside bundles of KANU votes, and then tying them in bundles of 50 which would each be counted as fifty for KANU. Secondly, and most importantly, even after two recounts—which had been demanded as a result of discovering these malpractices, he said—the number of votes counted exceeded the Administration's figures of the number of votes cast. At this stage,

[43] Kaggia's house in Kandara is a plainly furnished, four-room dwelling.
[44] *Daily Nation* June 11th, 1966.

Kaggia said, he and his supporters had decided that there was no point in arguing further with the District Commissioner about counting, since 'it was obvious that the whole thing had been arranged'. He had left Administrative Headquarters, and after he left the result was announced.[45]

KPU suffered comparable defeats in the County Council elections, also held in June, a few days after the Parliamentary contest. The party put up five candidates in Kandara, all of whom were heavily defeated.

There are, plainly, considerable difficulties in regarding the Little General Election result as a reliable indication of the distribution of political support in Kandara. The extent to which possible electoral fraud distorted the results cannot be gauged, neither can the influence of the undoubtedly widespread intimidation of KPU supporters be assessed. And, in the absence of important data on social stratification, land distribution and commercial activity, it is not possible to quantify political support for the groups involved by reference to social strata or classes which had shown themselves to be more likely to support one candidate rather than another. Violence and fraud may well have resulted in the election seriously understating Kaggia's popularity; nevertheless, the political cleavages along class lines outlined in this chapter would tend to support the contentions of Cliffe and Koff.[46]

Re-emergence of Factionalism

By mid-1966, then, KANU seemed effectively to have resisted the challenge of KPU and to have consolidated its position at the grass roots as well as in Parliament. In addition, the party had by then established strong connections with government departments and non-government organizations—many of these connections a direct result of the sharp political polarization of 1965 and 1966. The Administration, particularly, had proved a valuable ally in the elections, and other government offices had been or were becoming more closely involved with KANU notables, both on a functional basis and, less tangibly, on the basis of shared norms about development and shared perceptions of politics. With the purge of the radical elements, much of the suspicion which had earlier characterized relationships between civil servants and politicians appeared to be subsiding.

[45] Kaggia May 25th, 1967. The District Commissioner said there had been 'problems' in the counting, but denied that the votes counted exceeded those cast. Kaggia, like 15 other unsuccessful KPU candidates, filed an election petition in the High Court challenging the result; all the petitions were dismissed without hearing evidence, however, on the grounds that the petitioners had not deposited enough security for the costs of their actions.

[46] See pp. 23 and 24 above.

Not unnaturally, however, the removal of the Kaggia threat precipitated new conflicts and tensions within the party which, aside from their other effects, tended to undermine the fragile solidarity between local politicians and government officers. Some of these tensions were not new—the differences between Mwaura and Kiano, for instance—but they had been of less importance while Kaggia remained a serious competitor for district power. In his absence, competition between the anti-Kaggia leaders became more public.

Reference has been made earlier to Kiano's aspirations to national prominence: these ambitions, and their partial fulfilment, had much to do with his political difficulties in Murang'a. Firstly, his pursuit of political power in Nairobi—as well as his duties as a Cabinet Minister—had led Kiano largely to abandon the role of 'local-boy' politician. This was, of course, not uncommon among Kenyan politicians, but references to Kiano's 'big house in Nairobi' and alleged neglect of his home area were far more often made about him by Murang'a respondents than about other district MPs. In this respect, he was compared unfavourably with Mwaura and Kaggia, both of whom had continued to live in Kandara during their terms of office. Certainly Kiano paid few visits to Murang'a, although he did own land in Kangema, his home division and his constituency before the abolition of the Senate in late 1966 led to a reapportionment of constituencies to accommodate Senators moving to the House of Assembly. Secondly, Kiano's power as a Minister, and his supposed favour with Kenyatta, were not altogether welcome: some of his followers felt that his influence had been used more frequently to buttress his own position in Murang'a against possible rivals than to secure benefits for his followers or for the district as a whole. His use of *Mzee's* influence to try and persuade Kaggia to stand down in 1963, his attempt to undermine Mwaura, and his use of patronage to further personal political ends were cited as examples. Kiano had used external political resources, in other words, without a substantial section of his following perceiving them to have had any wider benefit than to Kiano himself, thus depriving himself of one powerful argument in favour of his leadership.

The actual processes of conflict in the months following the rout of Kaggia were difficult to discover—indeed, respondents became less informative about Murang'a politics the more recent the events under discussion, not unnaturally, since these were in many cases still 'live issues'. It is clear, at any rate, that there was a concerted move by the other Kandara leaders to isolate Kiano soon after the Little General Election. Barely two weeks after the results had been announced, Gachago requested the Minister for Home Affairs to investigate a secret organization in Murang'a which included civil servants in its membership, and whose aim was to 'frustrate' KANU in future elections and eventually seize power. The existence of the group, he said, had been revealed during the County Council election campaign, and Murang'a leaders 'seriously feel KPU is behind this movement'.[47] The Murang'a leaders did not, in fact, feel anything of the sort, if indeed they believed that such an organization existed: the reference to the County Council elections was to Kiano's support for the single successful independent candidate in Kangema against the official party man. Gachago's statement could be regarded as an opening gambit, designed to establish the loyalty of himself and his colleagues to KANU, and to serve warning on Kiano's allies in the Administration.

Kiano evidently felt his position within the party to be deteriorating, and may have assumed that he could be unseated from the party chairmanship. On August 16th, he announced that a Murang'a District Leaders' Conference to be held on August 27th had been postponed until September 10th.[48] However, the meeting due for August 27th was not a leaders' conference, but a meeting of the executive committee of the district KANU branch[49]—at which Kiano may have felt his position to be in danger. A leaders' conference had indeed been called for September 10th,[50] and Kiano's statement appeared to confuse the two. But they were quite distinct: leaders' conferences, held in Murang'a as elsewhere in Kenya, were attended by prominent district figures, including KANU leaders, representatives of community development committees and co-operative societies, heads of government departments, and others, whereas the August 27th meeting was of course restricted to party branch officials. It thus appeared that Kiano, aware of the seriousness of the campaign against him, had sought to prevent the executive from meeting, and was confident that his Administrative allies (as well as the nature of the meeting) would prevent his opponents from acting against him at the leaders' meeting.

Gachago issued a statement on August 25th, attacking Kiano and asserting that the executive would meet as planned; no record is available of what transpired. On September 5th, however, the executive met again, and resolved that Kiano should be suspended from office. The committee said that he had failed to convene or attend their meetings—an evident reference to his actions in the preceding weeks—had been disloyal to KANU by supporting an independent during the County Council elections, had purposely created misunderstandings among branch leaders, and had 'attempted to use tactics involving some civil servants in party affairs'. The statement was signed by Kamau

[47] *East African Standard* July 8th, 1966.
[48] *East African Standard* August 17th, 1966.
[49] Kamau Njoroge May 15th, 1967; *East African Standard* August 26th, 1966.
[50] District Commissioner, March 4th, 1967.

Njoroge as acting chairman, Gachago, Mwaura and Wanjagi.[51] Kiano replied that the meeting and its decisions were illegal, since he as branch chairman had not called the executive to meet,[52] and his response was to bring the influence of the national leadership to bear in his favour, since this was his distinct advantage over his rivals. With the authority of the national executive,[53] he announced on September 8th that the KANU Murang'a Governing Council would meet the following day at national headquarters in Nairobi.

At the meeting under the chairmanship of Senator N. W. Munoko, national organizing secretary, the council decided that Murang'a leaders would desist from issuing controversial statements, and would work together in private until their differences were resolved. More importantly. it was established that Kiano was still chairman of the branch, and that the suspension by the executive was invalid.

The council meeting served to underline two critical factors in political conflict in Murang'a, which had not been apparent for some time. Firstly, pressure from the national leadership of the party was clearly effective in persuading the sub-branch and locational delegates to support Kiano. This pressure, no doubt, had several components— Kiano was seen to possess the national power and the influential allies he had always claimed, and the delegates, many of them relatively unsophisticated, were made to feel important by being summoned to headquarters to make their decisions, rather than ignored in the comparative obscurity of the Murang'a Country Club, their usual meeting place. At the same time, of course, farmers and rural traders may well have been somewhat overwhelmed by this environment and the important figures importuning them. But aside from these influences, the meeting served to emphasize the patron-client nature of the relationships between Kiano and the other MPs. Mwaura, Gachago, Njiiri and Wanjagi might have been capable of mounting a coup within the branch executive; they were not, however, able to count on substantial political resources when their action was challenged. Kiano, as well as having the KANU national leadership to call on, could make some claim on the loyalties and interests of local leaders, while the others, with the qualified exception of Mwaura, could not. Once Kiano mobilized his resources to fight back, his opponents were forced to concede defeat almost at once.

Mwaura, in fact, seems to have been the most willing to acknowledge that Kiano should be reinstated, and both he and his associate Mwangi Thabuni hastened to turn the debacle to their advantage by alleging

---

[51] *Daily Nation* **September 6th, 1966.**
[52] Ibid.
[53] Mwangi Thabuni April 6th, 1967.

that the group which wished to oust Kiano hoped to replace him with Kaggia on the latter's return to KANU.[54] Thabuni asserted that steps might soon be taken to rid KANU of 'destructive elements' whose ambition it was to destroy the district's good reputation.[55] With Njiiri, Wanjagi and Njoroge offering no resistance, Gachago (who, like Kiano, had not been present at the Nairobi meeting) had been effectively isolated. It was characteristic of Kiano's political style, however, that he apparently did not seek to get Gachago ejected from the KANU executive or from his post as Assistant Minister of Lands and Settlement: Kiano had re-established his dominance, and sought to move once more into the role of unifier of a divided KANU rather than act as the avenging victor.

A confrontation such as developed in July-September 1966 was probably inevitable in the wake of the national and local KANU upheavals in the first half of the year. Kaggia had been removed as a political force within the Murang'a party, and the more conservative section of KANU was unequivocally in control in Nairobi. In this new situation, Murang'a politicians were assessing new political alignments, testing the strength of opponents who had been allies but were now potential competitors for power and position, and probing the limits of political action.[56]

The Nairobi meeting had the effect of settling these uncertainties, at least for the time being, since the strength of the individuals and groups was put to the test and Kiano's leading role legitimized.

Murang'a politics had thus passed through three discernible stages in the period 1961-67. In the absence of some of the most prominent radical leaders, KANU had been a mass party which, although the ex-detainees were at a disadvantage, could nevertheless claim to be the expression of national unity, of Kikuyu reunification and Kenyan independence. There were indeed rivalries and differences within the branch leadership, but these seem to have been peripheral to the party's role in the immediate pre-independence era. With the return to district politics of Kaggia and other radical leaders, however, the norms of unity and rapprochement came increasingly under attack, as the social and economic tensions produced by the Emergency years found political expression in factions within the party—factions whose ideological tendencies (partly as a result of developments at the national level) ultimately became their most important distinguishing

---

[54] Ibid.
[55] *Daily Nation* September 12th, 1966.
[56] Several informants, for example, spoke of the 'confusion' over the KANU leadership as being the result of Kaggia's defection, despite the fact that Kaggia had not held any KANU office for a year, nor had his supporters.

criteria. A number of related factors prevented these ideological conflicts from finding expression in the separate political parties of the 'third phase' after the 1966 schism, however. The high political and economic costs of supporting the Opposition, the tighter political control from the centre—through the Administration as well as through the party—and the perception on the bulk of the district's population that KANU offered both security in their land and the chance (however remote in reality) of personal economic advancement.

With Kaggia and the KPU thus thrust to the sidelines, KANU could still claim to be the only representative political organization in the district—even if that claim depended on an unknowable proportion of the Kandara population being excluded from the political arena. As has been seen, however, the new factor in this situation was the stronger influence being exercised from Nairobi and Gatundu: the scope for factional competition had been narrowed by the control being exercised by the national leadership. The prizes available in intra-party conflict at the district level were thus restricted, and those available in other arenas—the co-operative movement, for example—became more important.

An illustration of the way in which central control operated is provided by the long arguments arising out of the abolition of Thika District, which before independence had been a white enclave of coffee and sisal farms in the midst of the Kikuyu Reserve. The conflict over Thika's future shed interesting, if fitful, light on the nature of Kikuyu politics, and on the subtle gradations of power within the Kikuyu establishment.

In 1963 the Boundaries Commission abolished the white County Council, dividing its former area of jurisdiction between Murang'a and Kiambu, with the Chania River as boundary. But while it had ceased to exist for local government purposes, in terms of central government administration it remained a district, with a District Commissioner continuing to exercise authority over the whole area known as Makuyu, as well as over Thika Town itself which, having municipal status, retained its own town council (it is less certain whether the DC Thika retained authority over the southern part of the former district which now fell under Kiambu County Council—the President's Office said he did not, while the DC Murang'a said he did). In mid-1966, this patent administrative anomaly was corrected by the Government, after a motion moved by Kaggia and supported by the other Murang'a MPs had been accepted. Murang'a politicians had argued that the retention of Thika District for central government purposes, aside from being anomalous, had had the effect of cushioning the settler interests in Makuyu from the decisions of the African Murang'a local authority. Makuyu was thus added to Murang'a as a fifth division, and the southernmost part became joined to Kiambu. Soon afterwards, however, the political effects of the transfer began to make themselves felt.

The prize in the conflict was control over Thika's KANU organization: the town had continued to possess a full party branch (where only districts and 'first-class' municipalities were constitutionally entitled to one) under the chairmanship of Dr James Munene, who had become chairman of the town council after the defeat of Senator J. M. Njonjo, a prominent member of the Kiambu establishment, in the July 1966 municipal elections. Soon after his election, Munene, who came from Murang'a and retained business interests in the district, announced a series of projects aimed at encouraging more industries to come to the town—which already had considerable investment and was the second largest town (after Nairobi) in Kikuyu country. He established himself as an able advocate of the nascent commercial and professional middle class, initiating action to clear the municipal area of squatters and give substantial help to African salaried staff (mainly through building loans and the provision of council housing 'of the better type'). He also advocated, as part of the plan for 'first-class' status, that the municipal boundaries should be extended, and that ultimately Thika should have a Parliamentary seat of its own. Senator Njonjo, however, claimed that Munene had usurped the KANU chairmanship unconstitutionally, and that he was in fact the chairman of the branch. There was considerable tension in the town between the rival camps, with each drawing on allies in Murang'a—Munene was supported by Kiano, but opposed by Mwaura, since enlargement of the boundaries would eat into Kandara.

In the early stages, it appeared that KANU headquarters supported Njonjo, a relative of the Attorney-General; in September 1966, however the Kiambu KANU branch announced that neither organization was correct in its claim, since Thika was only entitled to a sub-branch under Kiambu. In January 1967, the President announced that the chairman of KANU Kiambu, Arthur Wanyoike Thungu (a leader of the Presidential bodyguard), was right. Kiano and Munene adroitly responded that they had accepted this position all along, and that Munene's faction was in fact the sub-branch—a claim which was rejected by Kiambu, which conferred sub-branch chairmanship on Njonjo. The 'Murang'a interests' had thus been effectively excluded from access to Thika's important resources (with the partial exception of Mwaura), despite the fact that the bulk of the town's population and of its migrant labour force came from Murang'a. What was decisive was the President's personal intervention, and his support for 'his' district against Murang'a: the outcome depended on the access of politicians to the central party authority, which for Kikuyu affairs, at any rate, was the President himself—the KANU secretariat apparently played no part in adjudicating the conflict.

The Politics of Development

Thus far, the account of politics in Murang'a has concentrated on structural issues: it has stressed the political organizations involved, the groups engaged in competition, the manner in which critical engagements in the struggle for distinct political power were fought. So much was necessary to establish clearly the political environment of rural development in Murang'a, to indicate the setting and the actors with whom government agents were dealing in their attempts to gain access to and change elements in the district economy and society.

The chapters which follow thus represent a change in focus, away from the structures which were commonly accepted as political, towards those in which politics was nominally absent—i.e. the institutions of community development and of co-operative processing and marketing whose norms specifically excluded political activity either within or by the organizations concerned. That these norms did not count for very much is in part due to the mythical character of the claims to be 'above' or 'outside' politics which organizations are often prone to put forward in self-delusion or self-defence; in part, however, it was because they were particularly susceptible to being breached by the virulence of political conflict in Murang'a.

The completeness with which these 'development' institutions became politicized was not, however, due to some unique quality of Murang'a politics; it stemmed rather from the fact that the community development movement and the co-operatives possessed strategic resources which local political actors—both professional politicians and others—wanted to own or control, and from the fact that there was no effective way in which either administrators or members of these institutions could insulate or protect them from such political incursions. The metaphors of insulation and incursion are in any case somewhat inappropriate: as will become apparent, political conflict affecting rural development institutions was often a matter of internally generated conflict over what were perceived to be institutional issues, rather than attempts to introduce KANU or KANU-factional conflicts and actors into the institutional arenas concerned. Secondly, for the government officers there were important political requirements and constraints: their presence and their activities in the district in general constituted, of course, an important set of political facts in themselves, and their actions in particular circumstances were often partly dictated by political considerations, and had an immediate relevance to the outcome of local conflicts. In this aspect, too, the 'politics' of community development or co-operatives had little to do with professional politicians.

The politics of development in Murang'a, in some important

instances, thus only involved KANU and its factions at a relatively advanced stage. It will also become apparent, however, that the articulation of institutional or economic conflicts as *political* issues revealed much about the social basis of power in the district, and hence about the ethnic elite which dominate Kikuyu (and Kenyan) politics.

Chapter IV

DEVELOPMENT AND LOCAL POLITICS: THE ROLE OF THE COMMUNITY DEVELOPMENT OFFICER

Community development is more directly concerned with political themes, and more susceptible to local-level political influences, than many other areas of development activity. The norms of self-help and community development are those of popular participation, of the democratic control and utilization of resources, of a conscious effort to modernize attitudes and create demands and desires which were not present before. Community development administrators hope to instil an awareness, not only of 'community', but also of the individual citizen's relationship to the government, and of the responsibilities which both bear in the ordering of economic and social life (the fact that the picture drawn of this relationship by the development agent may be highly idealized brings its own problems, of course).[1]

These, however, are very general norms, and the actual programmes of community development agencies only rarely aspire to encompass them all—the 'lesson' a citizen learns from co-operating in the building of a secondary school or a health centre is a very partial one, and its effect only cumulative. At least in the short term, perhaps more important than the creation of a social consciousness which encompasses values closely concerned with political issues and the nature of

---

[1] For an excellent discussion of the norms of the community development movement, see Bernard Schaffer, 'The Deadlock in Development Administration', in Colin Leys, ed., *Politics and Change in Developing Countries* (Cambridge, Cambridge University Press, 1969) esp. pp. 203-6. For e.g. A. R. G. Prosser, 'Community Development and Its Relation to Development Planning', *Journal of Administration Overseas* Vol. VII, No. 3, July 1969, and the polemic between Biddle and Oxenham in *Community Development Journal* Vol. 3, No. 4 and Vol. 5, No. 1.

the political system, is the fact that community development programmes involve the formation of formal, localized groups with specific objectives and some economic resources. Particularly in rural areas, where few non-government bodies exist, local self-help groups or CD committees therefore offer both a training ground and a political arena for local political actors, and a potential constituency of organized support for local politicians.

The norms of community development will be examined later: at this point, however, it should be noted that Kenyan CD differed in emphasis from some other approaches. In keeping with its origin in the colonial period in such programmes as communal terracing, it carried strong administrative overtones (i.e. less emphasis on *'animation rurale'* and communal goal-setting, more on administrative control and identification of desirable projects), and the programmes and controls were seen as complementary to and subordinate to the requirements of economic planning.[2] It can readily be seen that the character of the programme—directed, bureaucratized and, as will be seen, bearing an uncertain relationship to other administrative functions at the district level—implied problems of accommodation and reconciliation for the community development officers responsible. It is these problems with which this chapter is in the main concerned, since they throw into quite sharp relief some of the major political dilemmas of development administration in Murang'a. The Department of Community Development in Murang'a was trying to cope with a number of different requirements—not only in terms of adherence to the rather high-flown norms of the CD movement, but also in terms of government emphasis on programme achievement and the maintenance of tight administrative control, and in terms of the realities of rural political power.

The Community Development Structure

Only two of Murang'a's community development workers at the beginning of 1967 were employed by the central government—Wilson Wahome, the District Community Development Officer, and his driver. Some other Kenyan districts also had an Assistant CDO on central government establishment, and this was the case in Murang'a in May-June 1967; Wahome was transferred on promotion shortly thereafter, however, and his assistant took over as CDO. Murang'a County Council, on the other hand, employed nine community development workers, three CD Assistants, a District Social Worker, a sports organizer, a clerk, a driver, and two messengers. All these (or rather the CDAs and the social worker and sports organizer) had

[2] See *Development Plan,* pp. 324-7, and Sessional Paper No. 10, p. 36.

district-wide responsibilities, under the supervision of Wahome, the CDO.[3]

Each Area Council (one per division) also employed a substantial number of community development workers: 24 in Kandara, 19 in Kigumo, 18 in Kiharu and 17 in Kangema, in the first quarter of 1967. Typically, the most senior Area Council Employee was a Divisional Community Development Assistant, with locational CDAs under him, many of them women mainly concerned with organizing wives under the aegis of *Maendeleo ya Wanawake* (Progress for Women—the government-supported organization which undertakes the training of women in diet, domestic hygiene, handicrafts and, latterly, birth control). Each division also had a least one adult literacy teacher, and several male crafts instructors.

Budgeting arrangements were correspondingly complex. Apart from paying the salaries and office and travelling expenses of the small staff actually on its payroll, the central government was not in fact committed to spend money every year on community development in Murang'a. In practice, of course, it did, by devoting small but regular amounts of money towards the running of projects under the CDO's direction. The great bulk of government expenditure, however, was discretionary: each district's progress in the establishment of self-help groups and the general implementation of CD policy was assessed at provincial level, and money allocated accordingly. Wahome explained:

> We don't actually see the cash. We are told by government HQ that there is so much, say Sh.23,000, for us. They send us a Permit to Incur Expenditure—a P.I.E. Then we see what is needed, and make out a Local Purchase Order and keep the materials in store, so that groups can draw on it, and the money is paid by the Government.[4]

The County Council, on the other hand, spent most of its contribution on recurrent expenses. Of the estimated total Community Development vote of £5,450 in 1966, some £3,000 was spent on salaries, travelling allowances and staff provident fund contributions; a further £1,000 was allocated to the running of UNICEF-donated vehicles for which the Council was responsible, and £200 to training courses for CD staff. Only £140 was devoted to self-help projects and the encouragement of

---

[3] The division of CD responsibilities, with the burden mainly borne by local authorities, derived firstly from the perception of CD as a development agency which did not require substantial government investment, and secondly from the 'ideological' requirement that, if it was to achieve its objectives, it should be as closely associated with local communities as possible. For a firm re-statement of this view, see Prosser, op. cit., esp. p. 213.

[4] March 1967.

handicrafts, and not all of this was spent. There were, however, contributions of between £250 and £350 each to sporting events, adult literacy and to the Government-sponsored district and provincial news-sheets.[5]

The Area Council, similarly, spent little in capital aid for community development. Apart from providing traditional dances and sports competitions, there was little expenditure which did not fall under the heads of staff costs and routine CD building maintenance. In 1965 (the last year for which figures were available) the Area Councils spent, on average just under £3,000 per annum each on CD. In Kandara, Kigumo and Kiharu this represented approximately one-third of their total budgets; in the case of Kangema it accounted for almost one-half.[6] In contrast, County Council expenditure on CD amounted to only about 0.7% of the total Council Budget.

The local authorities in Murang'a thus contributed little to the specifically developmental content of the Department's programme; what they did was to provide the personnel and the organizational network within which central Government funds and voluntary contributions were distributed.

The infrastructure provided by the Government and the local authorities was complemented by a voluntary structure, reaching in theory from the primary self-help group in the sub-location or village up to a District Community Development Committee, intended to supervise and plan the activities of self-help groups throughout the district in co-operation with the CDO. Self-help groups were usually started at the local level at the urging of a locational CDA, or after local people attended a chief's baraza, very often addressed by the Community Development Officer himself. A group would usually be formed for a specific project—building a nursery centre, levelling a bad feeder road, laying a water pipe—at a meeting in the village or at the market centre of a sub-location. A committee would be elected under Departmental guidance, and the group registered with the District Commissioner as a bona fide self-help group, which enabled the committee to receive a permit to collect money.

Although there existed in theory self-help committees at the divisional and district level, it was the sub-locational and locational groups which were the most effective. Few individual self-help projects covered a wider area than the location, and the planning and co-ordinating of divisional or district CD plans tended to be carried out by the Departmental officers rather than by volunteers deficient in knowledge and skills. Perhaps equally important from the viewpoint of

[5] Murang'a County Council Estimates 1966.
[6] Area Council Estimates 1965.

local leaders, the divisional and district committees commanded no financial resources, unlike the localized ones. Although the divisional and district committees apparently functioned during 1964 and 1965, no record of their meetings during 1966 and 1967 could be found, and the CDO himself, being unable to give the names of the current members of the committees, said he thought there were elections due to the committees sometime, and for the time being they were therefore 'in abeyance'. His assistant was somewhat more forthright:

> These committees aren't really much use to us. They don't know how to go about things, and so they don't plan, but sit around with their small quarrels about who has the best location. In any case these complicated arrangements look very nice, but a committee should have something to do, otherwise it's no good.[7]

It was apparent that they had become a liability to professional CD workers. During the first two years of independence, as far as could be discovered in interviews and somewhat sketchy minutes of meetings, the committees had operated mainly as arenas of competition between locations and divisions for a share in the 'spoils' of government counterpart grants to self-help projects. Inevitably this conflict involved pressure on CD workers and attempts to establish the committees as controllers, rather than advisers, of the bureaucrats. A comprehensive record of the behaviour of these committees during their active years would have been extremely valuable—not least for the light they might have shed on factional politics. Such detailed information as was available, however, was largely irrelevant to the themes of regional and factional conflict. It is clear, nevertheless, that factional as well as regional pressures on government officers were present: for example, in the Kandara divisional CD committee, there were repeated attempts by supporters of Kaggia to ensure that no self-help funds went to groups and committees known to be led by former loyalists, and at least one locational CDA was said to have been 'in the pocket' of a prominent ally of Mwaura.

At the beginning of 1967, there were 679 registered self-help groups in Murang'a, with a total membership of 45,387.[8] Many of these were inactive, having been founded and registered for a particular project and

---

[7] Assistant CDO, June 12th, 1967. Another factor militating against the effective operation of the committee at district level was the fact that the district CD committee in each district was supposed to become a sub-committee of the District Development Advisory Committees brought into being by the 1964-70 Development Plan. The DDAC's were generally unpopular with the Administration in Kenya, and particularly in Murang'a after the DDAC had been the focus of conflict between Kaggia and Kiano in early 1966.

[8] CDO's Annual Report for 1967.

having lapsed on its abandonment or completion. The CDO estimated that some 300 groups, with a probable membership of 20,000, were in fact active early in the year. For reasons discussed later, this too was probably an overstatement.

A great deal of the work done by self-help groups involved communal labour on members' *shambas* on a rota basis, with the group eventually carrying out improvements on each member's land. This activity did not, of course, qualify for government aid. There were also a large number of other communal projects which did not require money, either from government or from the groups themselves—charcoal burning, manure collection, woodcutting and so on. Another class of activity, carried out mainly by members of Youth Centres, was social service—caring for old people, cleaning their huts, digging on their shambas, and so forth, or doing heavy work for widows.

The projects which required voluntary contributions and central government aid were of a more substantial nature. High on the list of needs for which local communities sought aid were those which improved communications and facilities in the villages and sub-locations, notably the construction and repair of access roads, building bridges over small streams and culverts, laying water supplies to villages, and digging drainage sluices for farms and villages. Few of these projects required large injections of capital, but the little that they did need was often of critical importance. For example, an access road might be built by the group itself, using hand tools. But the group might need the use for one day of a Landrover with winch or a tractor for moving large rocks, and one or two lorry-loads of rough gravel to spread over low-lying sections for the road to remain passable during the rains. In more difficult terrain, of course, roads or drainage courses required more substantial sums for plant hire, skilled labour and materials.

The projects which required most cash, however, were also those to which local communities attached primary importance: the construction and running of schools (especially secondary schools), health dispensaries, and nursery centres.

The Politics of *Harambee* Schools

There can be little doubt that the people of Murang'a (and probably of most parts of Kenya) felt the provision of education for their children to be the first development priority. While improved farming methods or new crops might produce quite marked differences in styles of life, their effect might well be less dramatic and less immediately visible than a few years at school for a son or daughter: the disparity in opportunities between an illiterate father and an educated son, although not always welcome to the parents, was tangible and immediate. This is not to say that literacy or education was a source of wonder to Murang'a people: schools had been established in the district for more than half a century, and by 1967 well over half of Murang'a's school age population did in fact attend school for some period.

It is true, however, that the rapid spread of primary education after 1960, as well as the spread of awareness of the opportunities of education (in which community development workers had played a substantial part) had contributed to a markedly increased demand for educational facilities.[9] This increased demand, however, had been accompanied by an increase in sophistication: there was a corresponding awareness that more money, a better life and/or an escape from the rural areas was not guaranteed by the possession of a KPE (primary) certificate—which relatively few attained in any case—and that at least some secondary education was vital. As far as community development was concerned, therefore, self-help groups tried to set up secondary rather than primary schools, except in remote locations where children had a long way to travel to the nearest primary school. Particularly in 1965 and 1966, a large number of secondary school projects were started, encouraged by the President's exhortation to the people to provide for themselves the educational facilities they needed, where Government could not do so. This call struck a particular chord among the Kikuyu, of course, with their long involvement in independent educational endeavour, dating from the formation of the Kikuyu Independent Schools Association and the Kikuyu Karing'a Schools in the early nineteen-thirties. These *Harambee* schools, as they were known, presented one of the major problems for community development workers in Murang'a. As with other projects, self-help groups very often embarked on the building of a *Harambee* secondary school without even enough capital to finance construction, let alone to pay for teachers, equipment or other recurrent costs. The expectation, often encouraged by local politicians, was that government would be compelled to step in and take over the construction and running of the school.

> The trouble is that groups don't realize that schools and dispensaries are different from other projects. So we had a lot of trouble after the *Harambee* call, as people were building secondary schools and health dispensaries without troubling to find out if there was money for drugs, teachers and so on. People thought of *Harambee* schools as being like the old Independent

[9] 'In the old days of KAU and so on, it was the chiefs and some few educated who wanted schools for their children, because they knew what it could bring. Now all the people in Kenya know that you must have schooling, and we have got to make places.' County Education Officer, April 1967.

Schools of the colonial time, and they said 'Now our own schools are coming back. We must build as many as we can.'[10]

The problem was not confined to Murang'a. In November 1966, there were 200 registered *Harambee* schools in Kenya, employing about 1,000 teachers. It should be noted that this total represented only those schools whose communities had managed to raise the £2,000 required by the government since early 1966 for the school to be registered. The purpose was to ensure that *Harambee* schools would not be started without a minimum of capital to erect buildings, provide some equipment and have cash in hand for initial running costs.[11] But even this requirement had not solved the schools' financial problems: as an MP pointed out, the annual bill for *Harambee* teachers' salaries was of the order of £500,000, which meant that on average each group running a school was burdened with a salaries bill of £2,500.[12] These difficulties had led to insistent demands by MPs and local leaders for government to take over the schools entirely, or at the very least to take responsibility for payment of teachers. Only 21 schools had been taken over by the end of 1966, however, and there were frequent complaints in Parliament and at the local level that government, having initially urged the people to start schools, was now shirking its responsibilities in refusing to help finance them.

The Government's dilemma was set out by the Minister for Economic Planning and Development in the debate on the revised Development Plan, 1966-70.

> We expect secondary school enrolment almost to double during the Plan period—from 33,500 in aided schools in 1965 to 65,500 in 1970. To achieve this expansion, almost 3,000 teachers will be required by 1970, without considering the additional demand imposed by the unaided and *Harambee* schools. While it is anticipated that about 1,250 teachers will graduate from Kenyatta College and the University in this period, the supply will not meet the replacement and expansion requirements. . . . If in addition many *Harambee* schools are brought into being during the next few years, the staffing of them can only be accomplished at the expense of the existing schools—unless, of course, the communities employ unqualified teachers to fill these posts. While this might appear to be an alternative, I believe most communities would agree that it is not a realistic one. . . . The Government will do all it can in assisting *Harambee* schools, but it has been decided that no more such schools will be built in future

[10] CDO, March 1967.
[11] Parliamentary Report, November 1st, 1966, col. 1513.
[12] Mr Godia, Ibid. col. 1514.

without the approval of the Development Committee of the Cabinet.[13]

The statement by Mboya points to the major problem of the *Harambee* schools movement: how could the use of scarce national educational resources (let alone the resources of poor local communities) be justified on schools whose educational and hence economic value was open to serious question? Part of the answer, of course, lay in the fact that the encouragement of *Harambee* schools was not purely for educational reasons. Certainly it was initially assumed that *Harambee* schools would make a positive contribution to development by providing some schools in the rural areas where government could not—that they would remove part of the central administration's educational burden, thereby freeing resources for expenditure elsewhere. But unless one can accept that the Kenyan planners were astonishingly naive, and believed that self-help schools would in fact provide secondary education at no cost to government, one must look for further justification for the programme. Particularly in the rural areas, the construction and basic equipment of a school did not represent a very large investment—as the government's stipulation of £2,000 as the required capital indicates. The real expense, as Mboya indicated to the National Assembly, lay in the payment of teachers; and the gain for government when local communities did manage to pay for teachers was partly offset by the loss incurred in hiring overseas staff or drastically expanding teacher training facilities.

There were, however, rationalizations for *Harambee* schools which were ideological and political. The impetus to build self-help secondary schools was part of the wider ideology of communal participation and co-operation put forward by the President and KANU in the first years of *Uhuru,* and it was only natural that the *Harambee* ethic should be extended to the area of education, which the population clearly regarded as an urgent need. At the same time, encouraging local communities to build their own schools helped the government, however temporarily, to cope with political demands for education which it was unable or unwilling to meet—and, particularly in Central Province—provided a solution which was very much part of a long-standing tradition of independent, locally-financed schools.

But if *Harambee* schools were quickly seen to incur substantial economic costs, in the form of a drain on teaching resources and on the small capacity for self-help of local communities, they also became something of a liability in political terms: the difficulties and in many cases the outright failure of *Harambee* secondary schools inevitably had repercussions on community development programmes and the propa-

---

[13] Parliamentary Report, July 5th, 1966, col. 1388-9.

gation of the self-help ethic,[14] and led to the demands, referred to above, for Government to take over the schools.

The £2,000 government requirement was a first step towards control; Mboya's statement that the Development Committee of the Cabinet would in future approve all new *Harambee* schools represented a more determined attempt to submit the schools to the exigencies of central government planning and cut down on the waste of resources. It is probable that the government also felt that the pressures on them to assume responsibility for running the schools might ultimately become irresistible, and so they should ensure that new schools should at least be rationally placed, adequately built and so on. The need for careful siting and provision of recurrent finance was continually emphasized by government spokesmen at rallies and *barazas* in rural districts in 1967.

In Murang'a at least, however, the control measures did not seem to have been very successful. The capital requirement, as far as could be discovered, was strictly complied with by the County Education Officer, who was responsible for recommending the registration of *Harambee* schools; the CDO, too, was at pains to ensure realistic planning by self-help groups, although he was hampered by the fact that groups which managed to collect an impressive initial sum were not necessarily able to maintain their performance year by year. The responsible officers in Murang'a did not, however, refer proposals for new schools to the Development Committee of the Cabinet, nor were they aware that they were supposed to do so. Neither the Education Officer nor the CDO had on file any circular stating that this should be done, nor that decisions to start schools (in the case of the CDO) or to register them (in the case of the Education Officer) should be referred to their provincial or national superiors, although their own decisions in these respects were communicated to headquarters in monthly reports after the event.

Thus two new *Harambee* schools were completed and registered in the second half of 1966, after the Minister's statement in the Assembly. By the end of March 1967, three more secondary schools, at Kibutha, Kamahuha and Kiruri, had had their applications for registration approved and were planning to open that year, although the relevant groups had not yet completed construction. Two more schools, at Kairu and Gachanjiru, were under construction, but had not yet furnished the Education Officer with proof of their financial standing.[15] A further secondary school, at Weithaga, was then under

---

[14] E.g. 'One big difficulty is that these people get discouraged and don't want to go on when the schools can't function because they haven't got money for the teachers. Then they start all the talk about government should be providing for them.' Assistant CDO, June 12th, 1967.

[15] Murang'a County Education Committee, Minute 10/67, March 22nd, 1967.

discussion, but was delayed by a dispute involving pressure on the Anglican Bishop of Mount Kenya to close the small primary school at Weithaga Mission and allow the *Harambee* group to open a secondary school in the building.[16] The plans afoot in Murang'a in 1966-67 are sufficient to indicate the scale of the problem; in administrative as well as financial and educational terms: schools continued to be built, despite the fact that by April 1967 there were already 24 *Harambee* secondary schools in the district, only seven of which were deemed by the educational authorities to be adequately staffed and run with minimum competence.[17]

Many of the *Harambee* schools in Murang'a were started at least partly for political reasons—as indeed were many other self-help projects and communal groups. Much of this activity is not particularly significant: it is to be expected that political leaders at the local level would perceive advantages in being associated with desired improvements. Two aspects of the 'political' nature of community development are worth examining, however: firstly, certain projects were started by local politicians in the expectation that representatives of the local communities concerned would be able to manipulate Government, the Community Development Officer or the County Council into taking over the project or into providing financial assistance. Secondly, in Kandara at least, *Harambee* schools and self-help activities in general had, since 1965, become increasingly involved in the political conflicts between local leaders.

The general expectation that Government would or should eventually take over the running of communally-built schools was certainly present in Murang'a, and some secondary schools had in fact been started in that expectation. The most reliable examples concerned two schools in Kangema division, in locations 14 and 19. In each case, the initiator of the *Harambee* school group was one of the councillors for the area—both of them members of Kiano's following. They were said to have started school building activities on the understanding that Kiano, as a Minister and the MP for the division, would be able to

[16] Minute 11/67, and County Education Officer. The dispute was unresolved by August 1967. Aside from the wish of some local people to retain the primary school, there were also attempts to persuade the church to open a secondary school of its own at Weithaga, instead of merely providing facilities for the *Harambee* school.

[17] USAID Education Adviser, Murang'a, based on provincial inspector's report. It is interesting to note that the CDO asserted that 'all the schools are running well'. The scale of the problem on a national scale can be gauged from the fact that the number of independent secondary schools for African students rose from 41 in 1960 to 601 in 1968. See John Anderson, 'Self Help and Independency: African Education in Kenya', *African Affairs*, Vol. 70, No. 278, January, 1971.

secure intervention or financial assistance from the Ministry of Education.[18] Kiano had not done so, however, by August 1967.

These pressures to build *Harambee* schools, stemming as they did from deeply felt and powerfully articulated communal needs, imposed considerable obligations on local political actors to be seen to deliver the goods. When schools were started and subsequently delayed or abandoned through lack of funds and expertise, there was a corresponding impetus for local leaders to shift responsibility onto government or its representatives in the district. Inevitably, local representatives tried to bring pressure on the CDO, who was perceived as more open to pressure and less secure than the County Education Officer, whose responsibility only became relevant when a school building project was far enough advanced for the group concerned to apply for registration. These influences, and the roles which the CDO evolved to deal with them, will be discussed below. At this stage, however, one further innovation by local politicians to deal with educational demands should be examined, particularly since it illuminates one aspect of the political divisions in Kandara.

Kandara had initially been the centre of a very vigorous school building programme. A large number of *Harambee* schools were built in 1964 and 1965, many of them evidently started without the knowledge of the Department of Community Development. Some schools were, however, approved by community development workers in the division, and construction was planned in the usual way—formation of a self-help group, collection of funds, and construction by communal labour under the supervision of CD staff. There were, however, a great many others which were started by locally prominent individuals without reference to the CDO, and which very soon ran into considerable difficulty. Thus the CEO estimated that, in the peak *Harambee* school-building period of late 1965, some 30 or 35 schools were under construction, none of them under CD auspices, and none of them having fulfilled either the £2,000 capital requirement or the standards of building and facilities demanded by the Education Department for registration.[19]

It is clear that in many cases the 'non-official' schools were encouraged by members of the Mwaura faction, no doubt as a means of bringing secondary education to the rural areas, but also to recruit support against Kaggia and his followers. According to one CD worker in Kandara, the schools were locally known as 'Ndirira schools', and one in location 3 was in fact officially named the Ndirira Harambee

---

[18] In the case of the school in Location 19, this version was confirmed by the councillor concerned—Mr Kabiri Mshugu—in an interview on March 21st, 1967. He refused to say, however, whether Kiano had consented to the arrangement beforehand.

[19] March 1967.

Secondary School, before it closed through lack of funds in early 1966. In a few cases, notably in locations 4 and 5, schools were started at the initiative of politicians who supported Mwaura, prominent among them Councillors Samuel Gachau and Jasmel Kariuki. For the most part, however, the organizers of *Harambee* building programmes seem to have been members of primary school committees. These committees, as has been mentioned earlier, constituted an influential section of Mwaura's support: during the Emergency, the committees were composed of (mostly Christian) loyalists and Home Guards, many of whom had retained their positions. Even in those schools where a substantial change in committee membership had occurred since the Emergency years, committeemen tended to be more prosperous and/or educated than most people, and therefore more likely to be hostile towards Kaggia.

In the building of self-help schools, as in most CD activities in Kandara, the political conflicts in the division rapidly made themselves felt. Initially, there was some attempt by the Administration, at the prompting of CD workers and at a time when the Administration did not yet have the authority from above to act against Kaggia in any way, to persuade members of the two factions to sink their differences, for self-help purposes, in the spirit of *Harambee*. That this effort was totally without success is ascribable in part to the militancy of Kaggia himself, and to his feeling that Government was attempting to evade its development and democratic responsibilities by 'hiving off' popular involvement into CD activities, while not allowing the opportunity for genuine mass involvement in the planning and development process. (This is a somewhat blunt and possibly oversimplified statement of Kaggia's position: nevertheless, he often referred to CD as a 'sop' which did not make up for what he felt were the anti-democratic tendencies of Government development policy). In part, too, the failure of co-operation in the crucial period of late 1964 and early 1965 stemmed from Mwaura's position of weakness following Kaggia's assumption of the branch chairmanship of KANU, and from the former's need to maintain and improve his political position in Kandara. The failure was described by Kaggia:

> When this was started, you see, I said specifically that we are not opposed to any building of schools, but certainly I'm not going to support this kind of school without any planning, because the government was not prepared to take over these schools, they could not even give us any guarantee that they would be taken over, and as the shortage here is mainly secondary schools, for us it is not easy to build all these schools, and run them, staff them, and so on. So I put two conditions that I will support this school building if they are planned and if it is agreed that in a certain

locality we must have one or two, then before we finish that we shouldn't start another one. That was the first condition. The other condition—I said this must be removed from politics. I said I am not going to allow people to go and support a project with my approval which is going to be used against me. And to see that this is not used by any politician, we must see that if it's a location school, the whole location must be called to select a committee which is going to run the school, instead of having two or three people just monopolizing the school and using it for their own ends. So this was not accepted, as most of the people who were starting the schools were my opponents, and they refused our conditions and so we refused to participate.[20]

In this Kaggia had a clear moral advantage, in that by calling for popular participation and the election of school committees, he was in fact abiding by the norms of community development. There is little doubt that Kaggia and his supporters would have emerged triumphant from such local meetings in nearly every location in Kandara: not only was Kaggia a popular MP (in spite of his dismissal from the government), but he was also at the time chairman of the KANU district branch. Mwaura, by the same token, could not allow his influence over the committees to wane at this crucial time, when his faction was engaged in its (later successful) effort to oust Kaggia from his position.

Kaggia and his supporters undoubtedly played a major role in the failure of many schools in Kandara after the collapse of attempts at co-operation, but it was not solely due to his hostility that they failed. From the outset, there had been little chance of many of the schools succeeding: the lack of liaison with the community development workers and the opposition of the County Education Officer minimized their chances of success. It is clear, however, that Kaggia's campaign against the schools contributed to their failure by narrowing the base of potential financial support and by diminishing the political value of the schools for the pro-Mwaura people involved. Kaggia asserted that all these 'non-official' schools failed as a result of his boycott; the CDO and CEO said, however, that three of them had managed to keep going after a fashion, and their sponsors were in 1967 trying to bring them up to registration standard in the hope of getting assistance from the two departments concerned.

With Kaggia's defeat in the Little General Election, and the subsequent exclusion of his followers from the County Council and the Area Councils, Mwaura attempted to use his influence on the new councils to start new *Harambee* schools. In August 1966 he made

[20] May 25th, 1967.

application to the Kandara Area Council for permission to use two vacant council buildings, constructed during the Emergency as future sites for trade schools, as *Harambee* secondary schools. Obviously, if these buildings could be taken over at a low rental, the problems of cost would be far easier to overcome. Before receiving the council's approval, Mwaura, Mwangi Thabuni and Jasmel Kariuki applied for a licence to collect money for the proposed schools. The CDO raised no objection, and forwarded the application to the District Commissioner; it was, however, refused, on the grounds that no permission to use the buildings had yet been forthcoming from the Area Council. The Area Council gave its permission in February 1967, but by then Mwaura had apparently decided against persisting in getting a *Harambee* school started, since no new application for a licence was received by the District Administration.

Mwaura had decided, apparently, to establish a private secondary school in one of the buildings, and to that end had approached several Asian traders in Fort Hall town for funds. They refused, but Mwaura was later said to have gained the co-operation of an Asian businessman from Thika, and the school was formally opened in April. Kaggia immediately launched a campaign against it, saying that it was intolerable that an Asian should be allowed to exploit African taxpayers by using their council buildings to raise money. He alleged that students were being charged a fee of 2,000 shillings per year, and were not supplied with books.

Mwangi Thabuni, however, denied that any Asian was involved in the financing of the school, and said that it was 'a real *Harambee* school built by the people themselves'—a claim denied by the acting CDO and the Education Officer. Whatever the conflicting claims, however, the fact was that a school had been opened in the building, although not by a registered self-help group, and it was unlikely that money had been collected 'informally' from the local population without it coming to the notice of CD workers in the location or Administrative officers in the division.

What was not clear was Mwaura's motive in going to such lengths to open a school at the Area Council building in Kareti (and in continuing negotiations to use the other council building at Rucho). If it was true, as it appeared to be, that this was a commercial proposition and not a *Harambee* school, the fees would have to be higher and the political advantage to Mwaura correspondingly smaller, while any monetary gain would seem to belong largely to his Asian partner as the main investor. The reason for his persistence would seem rather to lie in his relatively minor status, both in Murang'a KANU and in national terms. He did not appear to have the political resources to deliver benefits to his constituency by using influence with government and, unlike Kaggia, he had not proved to be an articulate and effective parliamentary representative.

KANU and Community Development

The narrative above illustrates one way in which community development has become subject to local political influences in Murang'a, and in particular in Kandara. Education was the subject of most intense competition, with politicians attempting to bring benefits to their areas and to acquire prestige and support for themselves by encouraging and organizing the building of *Harambee* schools. The demand for health facilities, too, led to the building of a large number of dispensaries and health centres, very often at the urging of local leaders. The role of the County Councillors was crucial here: since the health centres fell under the council's responsibility, councillors could hope that dispensaries and centres, even if built without the approval of the CD Department, could be supplied with dressers and drugs if sufficient pressure was brought to bear in Council.

There is little doubt that this sort of exercise succeeded quite often in the early years of the Council's operation; by 1967, however, the Council's overextended finances and the uncompromisingly stringent attitude of the Ministry of Local Government compelled the Council to allocate funds and staff only to those centres previously approved. Thus the Health Committee decided in February 1967 to recommend that provision be made in the estimates for eight new dispensaries, six of them built by self-help groups, but three applications by councillors for help for unauthorized centres in their areas were rejected.

But as was suggested at the beginning of this chapter, perhaps more significant than the activities of local politicians involved in particular self-help projects, was the fact that self-help activities involved the creation of formal groups—and thus organized potential political recruits—accessible to local political leaders. After independence, the ideology of community development was closely connected with the norms of the ruling party, with its stress on communal co-operation, pulling together for the common good, and of national unity. Local KANU politicians could therefore argue a legitimate interest in CD, and a particular status in the organization of self-help activities and the making of decisions about the use of communal resources.

In Kigumo, Kiharu and Kangema divisions, however, the participation of KANU notables varied widely from area to area and from time to time, whereas in Kandara the involvement of KANU figures was close and constant—indeed, party activists were the moving spirits in probably the majority of projects. In the case of the other three divisions, the relatively low level of party activity was partly attributable to the lack of opposition to KANU as an organization, and before the formation of KPU to the lack of serious opposition to Kiano; even in the manoeuvring within KANU which followed Kaggia's departure in 1966, none of Kiano's opponents were capable of mustering a substantial following with which to oppose him—apart from Mwaura. Where councillors, local leaders or other activists were involved in self-help activities, it was most often the result of a strictly local threat to the position of a particular individual, which required him to reinforce his support in the locality.

In Kandara, however, there *was* a threat to KANU, since the core of the party in the division consisted of what had been the Mwaura faction: although a substantial number of Kaggia's prominent supporters withdrew their allegiance from him when he left the party, or in the period of erosion which preceded his departure, power within the local sub-branch remained with Mwaura and his colleagues. Kaggia's support, although very difficult to assess, was sufficient to ensure that KANU need fear autonomous—and thus potentially dangerous—organizations from arising.

The origin of KANU control of many self-help groups in Kandara lay in the factional struggles of 1964-65, and particularly in the activities of the Atiririri Bururi Union. To this extent, the argument in Chapter 3 needs to be qualified: the social origins and Emergency political allegiances of many school committee members, and the intensity of the factional conflict within Kandara, had meant that self-help activities in the division were politicized at an earlier stage, and at all times far more noticeably, than in the other divisions. The politicizing of various fields of development activity noted in Chapter 3 as following the arbitration of the Murang'a KANU leadership issue in late 1966 thus applies in reality to the rest of the district: anti-Kiano politicians sought to increase their influence in areas of social life where previously they had little—most noticeably, for example, in the agitation of Kandara notables in the coffee co-operative societies in 1967.

Ndirira's rhetoric, as Chapter 3 indicated, revolved around the themes of patriotism, national unity and self-help: more specifically, Ndirira propagated the view that the conflicts of the past, between those who had supported the colonialists and those who had opposed them, should be forgotten and buried in a new Kenya founded on hard work and individual initiative. The DC's summary of the Mwaura group's views, quoted earlier, as 'work hard, forget the past and buy land', is fair in that Ndirira's propaganda was broadly similar to the unifying themes of KANU, but laid more emphasis on the bourgeois virtues of self-achievement and private ownership. In Ndirira's terms, community development and self-help did not conflict with this ethic:

rather, CD offered a vision of 'socialism' which did not include the socialization of private property, but which at the same time offered some opportunity of advancement and the provision of services to the poor, who might otherwise have been hostile to the Union and its wealthier supporters. Mwaura and his followers were thus assiduous in supporting self-help activitites in Kandara; while these activities fitted in well with the group's general political outlook, they also perceived that it was essential to prevent Kaggia's supporters from extending their influence through CD organizations.

If Kaggia did not actually oppose community development work in the division, it is nevertheless clear why he sought to insulate himself by laying down a series of conditions to be fulfilled before he was willing to render support. His attitude over the *Harambee* schools issue has already been discussed; this 'obstructionism', as his opponents were quick to point out, soon extended over the whole range of self-help activities. Indeed, Kaggia's reluctance over self-help (which, as was pointed out earlier, was not solely attributable to Mwaura's influence in the local CD committees) furnished his enemies with important arguments against him during the first half of 1966, when he was fighting for political survival.

The Tactics of CD Administration

The complex of interests and activities described above, coupled with the administrative organization of community development in Kenya, imposed on the CDO a complicated system of behaviour in achieving departmental goals. The remainder of this chapter will be largely devoted to exploring the nature of the roles he appeared to be performing in Murang'a, and the perceptions and attitudes on which his behaviour was based.

The CDO during most of the period of observation was Wilson Wahome, who had been in that post in Murang'a since mid-1965. In June 1967 he was posted to Mombasa on promotion, and was succeeded by Mr Kimalel, a Kipsigis, as acting CDO. Kimalel had spent approximately two months in Murang'a under Wahome's guidance before the latter left for his new post.

While Wahome was not a native of Murang'a (he was born and raised in Nyeri) he was a Kikuyu, and had spent a long time, by Kenyan standards, in his Murang'a post. By the beginning of 1967, then, he was to a considerable extent integrated into the local community, well-known to administrative officers and politicians in the divisions, and thoroughly versed in the informal subtleties of his job. Wahome offered an interesting contrast to Kimalel, the non-Kikuyu newcomer, who had to establish contact with key figures in the Administration and in the rural areas, and to explore the limitations of his office. Where Wahome's behaviour followed a well-established pattern, so that even seemingly quite novel problems could be routinized by applying known criteria and previous experience of somewhat comparable situations, Kimalel was consciously innovating to cope with situations which he could not have anticipated.

To take an example: the chairman of a self-help group in Kangema complained to Wahome, through the local Community Development Assistant, that other members of the committee had laid plans for a new project without consulting him (the chairman), and without a committee meeting being called to consider the proposals. He proposed, he said, to boycott the committee's work, and to ensure that no-one in his area co-operated with the self-help group. Wahome's response was to inform the chairman that he wished shortly to invite him to a meeting to discuss the working of all self-help projects in Kangema, and it would therefore be unfortunate if he no longer had first-hand knowledge of the situation in his area; at the same time, he ensured that it was suggested to the self-help committee by the local CDA that Wahome might find it difficult to continue to disburse government money designed to foster the spirit and practice of *Harambee* if the group was to act directly contrary to that spirit. Wahome explained his action as follows:

> You see, these people are always having some conflicts, but we must see that these do not get out of hand. Most of the time it is a very small thing. . . . Here, it is just that Kamau thinks he has no authority, so he is angry. If I tell him he is then going to have more authority . . . he will be happy, and the others will work with him because they have some important projects that will need our help.[21]

Kimalel's solution, when the situation was put to him on a hypothetical basis, was to say that he would have gone to the location and held a meeting where the committee would have been reminded of their social responsibilities, and of the need 'to obey the President's call of *Harambee*'.[22]

The point to note is not so much that Wahome's tactic was successful, whereas Kimalel's would probably not have been. More important was the fact that Wahome was able to categorize the Kangema incident, to apply known formulae to solve the problem—in other words, to apply pragmatic rules which he had evolved for dealing with a *class* of cases of local conflict among self-help activists. Kimalel,

[21] May 1967.
[22] May 1967.

on the other hand, could not do so, and was compelled to fall back on the general norms of community development.

Any Government officer, of course, develops patterns of behaviour to 'fill the gaps' left by training and the orders under which he operates: Wahome's duty, for example, was to promote the formation of self-help groups led where possible by 'well-known and responsible' local figures. There was much room for manoeuvre, and the practices Wahome adopted were to a large extent the product of restraints imposed by political considerations.

Thus he actively discouraged chiefs, sub-chiefs and headmen from campaigning for the chairmanship of local self-help groups, partly because he was concerned to emphasize the voluntary and non-official character of the CD programme, but more particularly because of the unpopularity of these officials, which was both a remnant of the colonial period (since a considerable number of chiefs had retained their positions since pre-independence days) and a reflection of their continuing responsibility for some local law enforcement and for the collection of tax.

Secondly, he tried to prevent politicians from becoming too closely associated with self-help groups, at least in official positions on the committees. This was far more complicated, since Wahome had at the same time to ensure that he retained the co-operation of the politicians—notably endorsement of particular projects at local public meetings. Part of the reason for Wahome's reluctance stemmed from the feeling, prevalent among Kenyan servants, that politicians were meddlers who hindered the efficiency of government and slowed the progress of development. More immediately, however, he felt that while there might be some advantages in getting an important political figure to chair a self-help group, any such gain could only be in the short term.

> You see, very often these chaps want people to think they are very important, so they will get a *Harambee* group going and it will work fine for a while. But then if they beat their opponent, or if they see it is not getting them anywhere particularly, they will just give up, and the self-help spirit suffers. Because people then think they are there only for politics, to get supporters, and not for the good of the country. So our policy is that we want their help, but we want ordinary farmers and location leaders on the committees, who live there and are not interested to go off to Nairobi and become big shots.[23]

This strategy was by no means always successful: as was noted earlier,

---

[23] May 1967.

there were frequent instances of local politicians taking the initiative in self-help projects, very often to achieve precisely those goals which Wahome opposed. And, of course, he had been unable to contain the very strong pressures in Kandara which had resulted in the politicization of the greater part of the self-help effort. Nevertheless, he had succeeded in part in warding off political encroachment on the work of his department—partly by the application of rules about the nature of the political process, and partly through the use of the District Commissioner's and the County Council's authority. Discussion of this latter factor must involve an account of the Community Development Officer's role within the central government hierarchy and within the organizational apparatus of the County Council.

Although community development is assigned an important developmental role in government documents such as the Development Plan, the Sessional Paper on African Socialism and the National Plan for Community Development, in Murang'a at least other officers ascribed to it a low status. The CDO was described as 'the most junior department head',[24] and few officers seemed able or willing to define any clear CD role in the development process. In some cases, self-help was seen as a form of charity,[25] with the department as a welfare agency organizing projects which did fall into the category of 'real' development, but which nevertheless made a marginal contribution to the well-being of the people. At its highest, CD was seen as creating an infrastructure within which 'real' development could take place, while at the same time providing an outlet for potentially dangerous discontents. Thus the Agricultural Officer's assessment:

> Community development is really quite useful to us—you see it gets people to know what is required of them, because they are organized into all these little groups, and they are told about terracing and so on. But it's up to us to come along and show them how to develop. . . . I would say the Community Development people are like people who run ahead to say what is coming. They go ahead of us to prepare the way, to make opportunities and so on. . . . Also, you must remember that it's hard to explain to these people that everything must come slowly and by a lot of hard work. They just expect the government to do everything for them right away. So self-help lets them do something for themselves, and that makes our work easier, because then people are not saying, 'Where is our development? They have failed us.'[26]

Needless to say, these views of the role of community development

---

[24] Agricultural Officer.
[25] An Administration official.
[26] Agricultural Officer, May 1967.

were not shared by the CDO and his staff; nevertheless they bred a sense of insecurity and a corresponding defence against deprecation of the Department's importance. In Wahome's case, his concern to enhance the status of his Department (and, by inference, his own standing within the district bureaucracy) involved the cultivation of a special relationship with the District Commissioner—or at least the appearance of such a relationship.

The organization of self-help facilitated this: the DC had to call on Wahome for advice in deciding whether to grant licences to groups wishing to collect money for self-help projects or to use government buildings, or licences to hold meetings connected with CD activities. In addition, Wahome made a practice of routing his requests to other departments for specialist help through the District Commissioner, although neither government circulars nor the DC himself demanded that he should do so. Thus, partly because of the nature of Community Development administration and partly through Wahome's own choice, the Commissioner was in close and frequent contact with the CDO, and had an intimate knowledge of the work of his Department—far more so than in the case of the other departments, where it seemed that the DC only became involved in detail when important political questions or issues of public order arose.[27] It was very difficult to assess how far Wahome had succeeded: his own view of the relationship as 'friendly and very understanding' is not necessarily correct. Nevertheless the DC assigned more importance to community development than did other Government officers, and, as far as could be judged by his actions, assisted Wahome in procuring technical aid from other departments which was not always willingly forthcoming.

The advantages which the DC gained from such a 'special relationship' are less immediately obvious: it would presumably be desirable from his point of view to have an ally in the administration whose allegiance and obedience did not depend solely on the primacy in the district hierarchy accorded to the DC by government. Secondly, the CD Department had more contact with the public, and particularly with politicians, than any other department, and close liaison would therefore be relevant to the DC's function of political control.

Reference has already been made to the dependence of the CDO on the County Council, because of the council's responsibility for much of the staffing and financing of CD work in Murang'a. It is here that one might seek additional reasons for the relationship which Wahome attempted to cultivate with the District Commissioner. As in the case of

[27] A qualification should be made: DC's had a generally very good grasp of government activity in their districts through the weekly meetings of the district heads of departments under their chairmanship. These meetings were however for the most part concerned with strategy and liaison, not detail.

the central government apparatus in Murang'a, Wahome had also felt compelled to protect himself and his Department by ensuring that the Council would not use the great power it held over CD to his detriment. His strategy was to make himself, as he put it, the 'Council's right-hand man'. Wahome attended virtually every meeting of the full Council, and of all Council committees which had the remotest connection with community development, whereas other officers (with the exception of the DC, who was ex officio a member of the Council) attended only those committees which directly concerned them, and then only infrequently. Wahome's view of his role vis-a-vis the Council is revealing:

> I show them that I am interested in their work, and in the problems that the Council has to face. We work together, and try to see if there is a way out of the various things which are causing difficulty... I have become the Council's right-hand man. Always they call on me to advise them on all sorts of matters, and it doesn't matter when I am not on this or that committee, because they will just call on me to give a hand with anything that comes up. Also, when there are these small misunderstandings with our departments here (i.e. central government departments) I help them to sort things out.... So I think there is a very good appreciation between us, because they realize the good work that self-help is giving the district, and I am able to help with things they don't understand, and even to sort out some of the personal things the councillors come to me with.[28]

Allowance may be made, again, for exaggeration and for describing what may well have been relatively isolated instances as a regular part of his relationship with the Council; it was clear, nevertheless, that Wahome enjoyed considerable confidence among councillors. The purpose of this deliberate and uncommon cultivation of members of the local authority appeared to be threefold. Firstly, Wahome's active interests in the Council's work, and his personal relationships with a number of important councillors, tended to safeguard his staff and his budget from attack. Secondly, and related to this, his intimate knowledge of Council affairs and of important members of the authority tended to some extent to isolate community development from political pressure—a fact of which Wahome was well aware:

> It has happened a few times that one of the members is very angry that we haven't done something in his area, or sometimes that he has been kicked off a (self-help) committee or something of that kind. Then he has come along to the Council to make

[28] May 1967.

trouble and threaten us, but the other councillors know that this is just this man who is jealous, and that we are always fair in our dealings with everyone. But now if I had not been going to the Council all the time, and spending so much time in that hall (the Council Chamber) they might have listened and begun a campaign against us. Now, I can just go and have a word with Kamau (the chairman, Kamau Njoroge) and the whole thing is finished.[29]

Thirdly, the Council offered Wahome an alternative source of influence and prestige: while Community Development had low status in the eyes of other central government officers, to Council members, in terms of the Council's financial commitment as well as in terms of the political relevance of community development, it had considerable importance. There may have been more to it than that, although little concrete evidence other than Wahome's own view of his role can be adduced. Wahome saw himself as mediator between the Council and the government in Murang'a, and particularly between the Council and the DC. The relationship between the Council and the Administration had not been free of tension, and it is conceivable that both sides might well have found in Wahome an ideal mediator: more than any other officer, the CDO was dependent on reasonably sound relations between central and local authorities, and Wahome had evolved informal and semi-formal relationships in both structures which enhanced his value as a broker.

To attempt a summary of Wahome's style: his method of achieving departmental goals involved applying rules about the behaviour of Murang'a political actors based on a relatively long stay in the district—rules which enabled him to identify the types of project which would incur political interest, and the sorts of decision which would enable political conflict or interference to be minimized. Thus his actions vis-a-vis the County Council were designed to eliminate potential interference from one important category of politicians, and at the same time to increase his authority by making himself valuable to the Council as adviser and as mediator between it and the central government. As far as particular projects or areas of the district were concerned, Wahome's concern was to manage conflict engendered by the activities of his Department by distributing prestige among a wide section of 'secondary' local leaders, while avoiding prominent politicians and civil servants. This style could not always be maintained: in Kandara, where competition was fiercest, his Department had backed out of the disputes between the Kaggia and Mwaura factions, after an initial attempt to seal off self-help activities from the division's political conflicts. Wahome felt that Kandara represented something of a failure

[29] May 1967.

for CD, and had an acute appreciation of the implications of Mwaura's dominance of self-help:

> It's a difficult situation there. You see, the KANU group has now got the support of the self-help groups, or nearly all of them. Now it is difficult for us, because they are doing good work, and also they are the supporters of *Mzee* and the call of *Harambee* in the division, and Kaggia always wants to obstruct. But now we have this thing that is troubling us: sometimes these Mwaura people have caused some trouble, and the people get a bit dissatisfied with the way things are going. And then they think we are one with them (the Mwaura group), so in some areas some of them have gone to the KPU people with their complaints, and Kaggia says the government and Community Development are discriminating, and this leads to quite a lot of bad feeling. But now there is nothing we can do—we must work with the groups which are there, and they are the ones who want to develop the country in the spirit of *Harambee*.... It is always political trouble that causes our difficulties.[30]

Wahome's difficulty was that he was not faced with a number of isolated local conflicts, but with a division-wide political dispute which had involved the self-help groups, and which could not be dealt with by the methods he had evolved. Short of re-making the self-help structure in Kandara virtually from scratch (which would have involved more resources than he possessed, and in any case incurred unacceptable political costs) he had no alternative but to support the dominant group with money and advice—at the same time being unhappily aware of the potential future cost of that line of action.

Wahome's successor had a radically different approach to CD problems—partly as a result, no doubt, of his inexperience in Murang'a. It would have been extremely valuable, had it been possible, to see if and how Kimalel's attitudes and methods were modified by a longer period of work in Murang'a; as it was, he had been in post as Acting CDO for little over a month when field work ended. Kimalel had been posted to Murang'a district from training at the Kenya Institute of Administration; before training he had worked for Nandi County Council, and then as research assistant to an anthropologist. His view of the function of community development and of his own role was self-confident to the verge of arrogance: since his work in the field and his dealings with politicians had been minimal by the time this research ended, little more can be done than to quote statements which indicate the values which—initially at least—governed his approach to his work.

[30] May 1967.

I haven't really found any difficulty in not being a Kikuyu. You see, once again the people realize that I am in the government, and they must co-operate with me if they want to get help.

I think Community Development is becoming the most important department. In fact, we are swallowing up the other departments, because we are the people who *do* things with the people. You see, we will get things started, and then hand over to the other departments. And the people know, because now I think politics is not like it used to be in Kenya. Now people know that what they need is not politics like before, but to see what the government can do for them and that they must persuade the government to help them. And that is where we come in.

I'm not too worried about co-operation with other departments. This always works very well between us. . . . Anyhow, it is their duty to give us what we need, because the President himself has said that Community Development is going to develop the country. But I think before long we will have our own technical people, and we will carry things through from beginning to end.[31]

In one sense, Kimalel's attitude was representative of thinking among Murang'a civil servants: his impatience with politics in a representational or party sense, his assertion of the primacy of government (and of government officers) were typical of civil service reactions to political issues. Few government officers, however, felt confident enough simply to ignore or rebuff important politicians, perhaps because they had experienced the efficacy of political influence in Murang'a, perhaps also because their training and professional indoctrination had been less professionally oriented in the sense of a marked emphasis on the worth and power of government service.

Kimalel epitomized the 'bureaucratized' view of community development implicit in aspects of CD administration in Kenya: since local communities depended on CD officials for critical resources— licences to collect money, permission to use government- or Council-owned facilities, counterpart project funds—the administrators could define goals, choose projects and even control self-help organizations if they had a mind to. In fact, however, most CD workers in Murang'a were conscious of a need to avoid self-help becoming just another administrative programme: there seemed to be little of the paternalistic bullying which often characterized what passed for community development in the colonial period.

This could be called a matter of style, since the CDO still possessed powerful sanctions, however tactfully they were deployed; but in fact the relatively democratic, discussional style which Wahome employed

[31] Various conversations, May and June 1967.

stemmed from a genuine commitment to the democratic norms of community development, as also from a consciousness of his own vulnerability. The resources he possessed were largely only in relation to those of poor local self-help groups, and capable of dealing only with a relatively low level of pressure. Intermittent localized conflicts could be managed and controlled in a way which did not involve abandoning the requirements of mass involvement and administrative control; given intense conflict as existed in Kandara, however, the Community Development Department could not prevent the erosion of the notion of communal participation—indeed, once Kandara self-help groups had been effectively politicized, the Department was in fact strengthening Mwaura's control by giving them money and advice. This was not necessarily a bad thing in terms of immediate achievements—self-help groups in Kandara were rather better-organized than elsewhere in the district—but it did mean, as Wahome was aware, that administrative control had been diminished to the extent that CD had become a political resource reinforcing social cleavages, in contradiction to the *Harambee* ethic, in a manner he was powerless to prevent.

This fact is one illustration of the tensions implicit in the aims of community development in Murang'a—and perhaps in the assumptions of the community development movement in general. For the central government, CD offered a potentially useful and inexpensive source of economic growth and, it is safe to say, a convenient way of accommodating demands for development which would otherwise be difficult to satisfy. It demanded, however, institutional arrangements which would enable it to relate effectively to the rural population (and also minimize costs to central government) while ensuring the retention of sufficient control to avoid situations which would be bad for planned development and which might also be unfavourable in their political repercussions (e.g. too many ill-planned, over-ambitious, uncompleted projects). Thus the splitting of CD responsibilities at district level between central government and local authorities, and thus too the small commitment of government resources to the Department. But weak institutions must spend a large part of their resources on institutional maintenance, and in Murang'a this meant not only the courting of District Commissioner and County Council and mediation between the two but, as in Kandara, accommodation to external pressures which involved the partial abandonment of CD objectives. In general, the Murang'a experience with community development is instructive. In the sorts of ambiguities involved in CD in Murang'a, for example, one might see the germs of contemporary patterns of self-help administration in Kenya: energetic, efficient at a certain sort of fund-raising and communal organizing task, and authoritarian in the extreme. The central importance of the Administration—of Chiefs and

DCs in particular—could not be more apparent, for very much the same reasons as encountered in Murang'a.

The politics of community development in Murang'a thus found expression in pragmatic adjustments to major pressures on the part of CD officials. Firstly, the organizational structure of CD (which reflected in turn its place in national development strategy and its political function for government) required that the CDO spent much time on maintaining access to specialist services and on safeguarding the integrity of his budget; to this end, he felt it necessary to act as broker between local authority and District Administration, or at least to appear to do so. Secondly, the implementation of community development programmes—and in particular the self-help schools programme—could and did result in CD resources being converted to the use of peasant political leaders. The word 'programme' in this context, in fact, conceals an important aspect of the politicization of community development: that its very flexibility, its responsiveness to 'community needs' while retaining bureaucratic control of key resources (such as licences to collect money), meant that 'programmes' were in reality the result of complex political interactions between CD officials, peasants, and local leadership groups.

The resulting mix of motives was not necessarily inimical to official ends—indeed, CD activity was in practice founded on the premise that leaders or would-be leaders would perceive self-help projects as conferring status and power on those who organized them Where these political aims came into conflict with bureaucratic norms (e.g. conflicts within self-help committees, or misappropriation or misapplication of funds) they were localized, and susceptible to pragmatic administrative and political solutions. Where political conflict involved (however crudely) identifiable socio-economic categories, however, and was thus no longer organized on a strictly parochial basis and was less concerned with the distribution of power and status within the CD structure itself than with larger questions of opportunity and allocation of resources, the resulting problems were no longer capable of bureaucratic solution.

In that respect, the case studies presented in this and the two succeeding chapters are of a piece in their emphasis on the primacy of politics in determining the outcome, or at least the longer-term significance, of the rural development policies discussed. There is, of course, nothing particularly remarkable in that, except as a corrective to the assumption in much development literature that, once away from the capital, it is administrative initiatives and bureaucratic ability to cope with 'obstacles to development' which are most relevant. In Murang'a, the administration operated in a context of intense political conflict over the available resources, and with a high degree of awareness of the significance of particular administrative initiatives for the groups affected. The really interesting issue is the forms which these political responses took, for they throw light not only on the structure of Murang'a politics, but on the trajectory of rural social change and the capacity of government to influence events in the rural sector. In the two chapters which follow, the emphasis is precisely on these limitations to bureaucratic power, and on the interactions between the local peasant leaderships and the ethnic elite in Nairobi which was ultimately responsible both for the formulation of rural development policy and for the character of administrative reactions to local political pressures in Murang'a.

Chapter V

COFFEE AND AGRICULTURAL DEVELOPMENT

The Kenyan government's development strategy identified expanded agricultural production as the principal means of economic development, and success in planning therefore depended in large measure on the government's ability to control events in the agricultural sector. Coffee is, of course, the major crop, and there is no immediate prospect of this aspect of Kenyan agriculture changing drastically.

> Within the last ten years its percentage share in total exports has been as high as 36% and never less than 17% ... coffee is still expected to account for 24% of the country's exports in 1970. However, due to restrictions on planting imposed under the International Coffee Agreement, any increases in coffee production after the Plan period will result from increased productivity rather than additional acreage coming into bearing, and coffee's share in total exports may be expected to decline gradually relative to commodities on which no such restrictions exist.[1]

Coffee was and is not, therefore, a 'development' crop: there can be no long-term government policy to encourage farmers to plant more and produce more coffee; rather the reverse. The development problem of the Kenya coffee industry, as is the case with a number of valuable agricultural export commodities, is not one of expansion of production but of careful limitation and quality control. Under the conditions imposed on Kenya by the International Coffee Agreement's quota system, the government had a overriding interest in being seen to pursue the stringent limitation of all new coffee planting and indeed, were it possible, the reduction of existing acreage.[2] Not only was it

---
[1] *Development Plan 1966-70* (Nairobi, Government Printer) p. 176.
[2] The crop seasons 1966/7 and 1967/8 were the first for many years in which world consumption requirements exceeded production, mainly due to low Latin American and Ivory Coast deliveries. See *Tropical Products Quarterly* (London) September 1968, Vol. IX, No. 3.

necessary for new planting of coffee trees to be limited, however—and in this respect the above quotation from the Development Plan may be slightly misleading. 'Increased productivity' could not mean getting more cherry per tree, because the quota system operates on the basis of the amount of coffee which can be sold in quota markets, and not on the number of trees or acres planted. The increased productivity which concerned the government was not therefore an increase in the tonnage of clean coffee, but maintaining and if possible raising the traditionally high quality of Kenyan coffee in order to gain the best possible return on a fixed tonnage quota. (A qualification is needed here: although during early 1967—the period most relevant to this study—this statement held true, the increasing incidence of Coffee Berry Disease after unusually heavy rains in mid-1967, an incidence still extremely serious in 1968 and 1969, led to a marked fall in Kenyan coffee production, giving rise to a need to increase the total output of Kenya coffee estates and smallholdings.)

If Kenya were to violate the terms of the Agreement, it would lay itself open to penalties from the international body—penalties which could include a reduction of its quota. It would still be possible, of course, to sell surplus coffee in non-quota markets—but at prices which ran, at the period in question, at about one-third less than quota market prices. Kenya's interests were therefore seen as best served by keeping the non-quota surplus as small as feasible, while at the same time controlling and upgrading cherry quality to preserve the domination by Kenya arabica of the lucrative mild coffee market.[3]

When Kenya joined the International Coffee Organization in September 1966, the country's quota was fixed at 43,970 tons; by March 1967, it had already been cut to 41,085 tons. The crop for the 1966-67 season, however, amounted to just under 55,000 tons, leaving some 20% of the entire output to be sold on non-quota markets at lower prices.[4] The overproduction was the result of the extremely rapid expansion of African coffee growing in the early Sixties: African coffee acreage trebled between 1961 and 1967 to about 130,000 acres, compared to 75,000 acres of estate-grown coffee, most of the latter owned by the white settlers or European-dominated firms.[5]

Control of Coffee Acreage

Initially, African coffee planting standards were carefully controlled by the Department of Agriculture, but the control system broke down

[3] Plan, p. 177.
[4] *Kenya Coffee* (Nairobi) March 1967 p. 92; Coffee Board of Kenya *Annual Report* for 1967; *Tropical Products Quarterly* September 1968.
[5] Department of Agriculture Press Statement, June 4th, 1967; cf. *Plan* p. 367, which gives the figures at November 30th, 1965 as 129,557 acres for small-holders and 80,118 acres for estates.

completely in the planting rush of 1963-64, when notice of intention to restrict planting under the I.C.A. was given to growers. In 1964, expansion of coffee acreage was prohibited, and in 1966 new planting was limited, in theory, to infills of 6%—that is, growers were allowed to buy seedlings to replace old or diseased trees up to 6% of their total number of trees. In January 1967 the infill quota was cut to 2%.

Given these stringent prohibitions, the crux of the problem was obviously enforcement, and in 1966 the government promoted legislation setting up the Coffee Authority, whose task was to improve and control African-grown coffee only (the Authority's scope was limited to coffee grown by co-operative society members), and providing additional powers to control the industry by declaring coffee to be a 'Special Crop'. The government's strategy was to order, early in 1967, that nurseries attached to estates and to co-operative societies were permitted to distribute only enough seedlings to cover the 2% infill allowance. The remaining seedlings were to be destroyed by inspectors of the Coffee Board of Kenya, and compensation paid at the rate of 20 cents per seedling. Furthermore, no nursery was to sell seedlings without the production by the buyer of a grower's certificate, and receipts were to be issued as a check on purchases. Coffee trees planted illegally would be uprooted without compensation, and illegal planters could be prosecuted.[6] Some uprooting of African coffee, although on a small scale, was in fact started in Kisii in March-April 1967, and a little later in Murang'a and Kiambu. More vigorous action was taken against the estates, however: in Makuyu (southern Murang'a), Kiambu and Kitale, coffee on 'marginal or neglected' estates was uprooted in May and June, and some thousands of trees on estate nurseries were burned.

The scale of the acreage problem, as it then stood, may be judged by doing a crude calculation of 'excess acreage' on the basis of the surplus tonnage (i.e. coffee tonnage surplus to the quota) produced in the 1966-67 crop season: from the figures quoted at p. 84 above, it will be seen that approximately 40,000 acres of coffee would have had to be eliminated to reduce the 11,000-ton surplus to zero. The government's own figure, however, was even more alarming: the Minister of Finance estimated in February 1967 that production from 58,000 acres would have to be eliminated to bring Kenya's gross output down to what the country was able to sell through the International Coffee Organization.[7]

This government statement, extremely difficult to reconcile with production figures, was characteristic of the defensiveness of official spokesmen on the coffee control issue at the time. It is arguable that policy on coffee in 1967 was still dominated by past experience, when

---

[6] See monthly issues of *Kenya Coffee*, November 1966 to March 1967.
[7] Speech by James Gichuru to the Annual Coffee Conference, February 3rd, 1967. Reported in *Kenya Coffee* February 1967.

the interests of the white coffee producers had been paramount. Maintenance of this policy from colonial times would also have been assisted by the fact that the Ministry of Agriculture, as well as being headed by a settler Minister, drew heavily on European expertise, as did the Coffee Board of Kenya. Certainly the government's insistence on the importance of quota markets tended to support the propaganda of the estate owners that very little coffee could be sold in non-quota markets. The government was, naturally, anxious to maintain coffee revenue, and high cherry quality coupled with quota-market selling was seen as the most appropriate means.

From the estate owners' viewpoint, however, an important rationale was that prices for non-quota coffee were lower, and hence average returns paid to growers would drop, with high-quality producers (predominantly estates) consequently suffering from a larger proportion of their crop being sold in non-quota markets. Kenya's strict adherence to the ICA thus detracted from the full potential of non-quota markets being explored, to the benefit of the estates but to the potential disadvantage of most existing African growers and of all would-be coffee growers, for whom coffee, even at a lower rate of return, would still have been an attractive farming proposition. The new Development Plan issued at the end of 1969, however, showed that substantial re-thinking had taken place: despite the fact that Kenya could hope to sell far more coffee to ICA markets because of the adverse world production conditions of the intervening years (reflected in the fact that the ICA quota for Kenya had actually been increased to 47,600 tons for 1968-69) the Plan expressed the hope that there would be a substantial increase in non-quota sales, especially in the Soviet Union, Eastern Europe and Japan. In 1967, however, the government was much more single-minded in its encouragement of quota-market sales, so much so that defences of their policy appeared occasionally to lose touch with reality completely: the Assistant Minister for Agriculture claimed in June 1967, for example, that even if all 75,000 acres of estate coffee were uprooted, Kenya would still have difficulty in selling all the coffee it produced.[8]

Co-operative Reform

Aside from planting control measures, coffee growers were also affected by government policies on co-operative reform: legislation to improve the administration of the co-operatives was largely drafted as a response to coffee control and marketing problems, and was seen as complementary to plans for raising cherry quality and limiting acreage.

[8] *Daily Nation* June 7th, 1967.

A second problem is the deterioration in management of many of the co-operative societies which play a vital role in the industry by virtue of their responsibility for buying and grading smallholder cherry, pulping and drying it, and distributing the payout from the marketing authorities. The societies' governing committees have become lax in grading members' cherry, thus destroying the incentive to produce quality coffee; they are tardy in rendering financial accounts; and some of them are frittering away 50% or more of members' proceeds on wasteful recurrent expenditure or urban land speculation and other projects unrelated to members' interests.[9]

Conditions within the co-operative movement in Murang'a are the subject of the next chapter; much of the activity in the district in 1967 to defeat government acreage control measures was intertwined with internal co-op politics, however, so that Murang'a co-operative affairs must also be discussed in this context.

The instrument for enforcing reform was the Co-operative Societies Rules, 1966[10], issued under the 1945 Co-operative Societies Ordinance. New legislation—the Co-operative Societies Act 1966—was passed late in the year, but it was the Rules which gave the immediate impetus to reform. The Act would have effect in the longer term, with provisions such as those empowering the compulsory amalgamation of societies, and more comprehensive financial provisions. The Rules gave to the Commissioner for Co-operative Development and his servants extremely wide powers of control over the affairs of primary societies and district co-operative unions, and also widened the scope of the unions' authority over the primary societies. It was envisaged under the Rules that the unions would co-ordinate all future co-operative development in their districts, and thus were to provide centralized accounting, marketing and supply services for their primary society members. They were entitled to inspect the books and premises of primary societies, and were made responsible for the appointment and terms of service of all primary society graded staff. The unions' chief officers became co-signatories, with district co-operative officers, to all financial transactions of primary societies.

Unions and primary societies alike were required to submit monthly trial balances to the Commissioner, to inform the District Co-operative Officer of all their meetings, and to refrain from acting on any resolutions until they were approved by the Commissioner. Primary societies were explicitly prohibited from providing for their members any of the services which the union already provided, and they were,

---

[9] *Plan* p. 177.
[10] Reproduced in Appendix.

88 Peasant Politics

finally, enjoined to diversify their activities into other crops rather than to form large numbers of single-crop societies. The government had thus responded to the related dangers of coffee over-production, declining quality and co-operative mismanagement with a series of measures which appeared to ensure effective central control of the major source of agricultural revenue. In Murang'a, however, the control policies fell considerably short of success.

The Murang'a Coffee Economy

Coffee is by far the most important cash crop in Murang'a, and coffee growing the major economic activity. In 1965 coffee earned £548,306 for the district; wattle, the next most valuable crop, brought only £75,000, and other crops were of far smaller value.[11] In 1966. however, the tonnage of Murang'a clean coffee sold doubled to 3,652 tons, and proceeds rose to £1,192,308[12], as large numbers of African growers picked cherry from their trees for the first time.

Coffee growers in Murang'a were organized into sixteen primary societies, all of them members of the Murang'a Farmers' Co-operative Union, which operated on a 3% commission on the gross proceeds of members' coffee. The coffee societies were the Union's main concern. Although there existed on paper 47 other co-operatives in the district (38 of them for the joint purchase of farms) most of them were virtually or totally defunct, and the Union paid them scant attention. Of Murang'a's estimated 95,000 landowners[13], about 25,000 were officially acknowledged as coffee growers—that is, they were members of registered coffee societies.[14] Members of primary societies elected their committees annually, and the primary committees in turn elected three delegates—one principal, usually the society's chairman, and two alternates—to the Union's management committee, responsible for Union policy. Each primary had a secretary-manager to administer its affairs, and was supposed to have a bookkeeper. Some societies employed clerks as well as the manual labourers who operated the coffee processing factories. The Union was likewise run by a secretary-manager, who had an office staff of about 15, including a qualified accountant, and also technical assistants, drivers, mechanics and stores staff. During 1967, a Finnish adviser on co-operative education and training was attached to the Union: he had succeeded two American Peace Corps workers in 1966.

[11] Murang'a District Annual Report for 1965, p. 32.
[12] Murang'a Co-operative Department Annual Report for 1966, p. 1.
[13] Murang'a Land Consolidation Annual Report for 1966.
[14] District Co-operative Officer, Murang'a.

Growers' Opposition

The opposition of Murang'a growers to Government efforts to restrict tree planting did not begin with the imposition of the 2% infill limitation in February 1967, although it was this stringent requirement which provoked political crisis. Murang'a growers had in fact been subverting coffee control since 1964, when the expansion of coffee acreage was prohibited. According to the Murang'a Department of Agriculture, between 1964 and 1966 the acreage under coffee in the district expanded—quite illegally—by 'up to 15%'. The accuracy of that estimate is impossible to assess, but co-operative society committee members were quite prepared to admit that substantial new plantings of coffee had taken place in that period without authorization.

The crux of the problem, as it was seen by Agriculture officials in Murang'a and in the capital, lay in the fact that there was no restriction on the *replacement* of coffee trees, and that this rendered nugatory general prohibitions on new planting. Since primary societies had their own nurseries of coffee seedlings, there was nothing to stop them selling seedlings to their members for 'infilling' old or diseased trees, and no effective check on whether those seedlings were actually used to fill in, or for illegal new planting. The 6% infill limitation imposed before the 1966 planting season was thus intended to close this particular gap in the planting control machinery.

The Director of Agriculture therefore allocated to Murang'a growers an infill allowance of 320,000 mature seedlings—i.e. about 600 acres of coffee. This figure was based, not on any census or even estimate of the number of trees, but on the acreage authorized when new planting was prohibited in 1964—20,661 acres. Before allowances were distributed among Murang'a growers, each primary society was ordered to prepare a register showing the number of coffee trees on each of their members' holdings, and giving details of trees over and under three years old, and of empty holes. Seedlings were then to be allocated *pro rata* to the primary societies by the Union, for planting during the long rains.

In the Murang'a context, the Department of Agriculture had committed almost every possible mistake in implementing the restrictions on infilling. Firstly, it was unrealistic to expect adherence to the infilling allowances when these were based on the by now fictional acreages of 1964. Both the local officers of the Department and the coffee societies were aware, of course, that much new coffee had been planted since then, but both parties had a distinct interest—as indeed did the central government—in not laying undue emphasis on the fact. The government was trying to adhere to the standards of the International Coffee Agreement, preparatory to formal signing of the Agreement later in the year, and therefore would not have welcomed public evidence of the partial failure of its efforts. In any event, the extent to which the central government was in fact aware of overplanting in Murang'a is doubtful: although the District Agricultural Officer (DAO) did inform his superiors late in 1965 that illegal planting had taken place, his warning was couched in the most general terms.[15] The DAO could scarcely be more specific, both because of the paucity of his own information and because of possible repercussions, since planting control was his general responsibility.

The coffee societies, for their part, had little choice but to reinforce the myth that only 20,661 acres were under coffee in Murang'a: while they had no intention of abiding by the 6% allowance based on that figure, the registers which they were compelled to prepare before receiving their allocation could not be allowed to show the excess. But even had the Department possessed accurate figures of the actual acreage in Murang'a, it is clearly unlikely that the 6% limitation would have been observed. The second cardinal error, in retrospect, was to attempt to implement an extremely unpopular policy without control over the critical resources. As a member of the Union's management committee succinctly put it, 'The Agricultural Officer was handing out pieces of paper, but we had the trees.' Since each coffee society ran its own seedling nursery to which its members had convenient access, the authorizations issued by the Department of Agriculture were of little effect: growers simply bought however many trees they wanted.

> After a while, in the long rains it became clear to us that there was nothing, *nothing* we could do to stop these fellows. Just a few officers could not run around 16 nurseries here in Murang'a, and then just run up to Makuyu, where the estates were also selling trees to our growers, and say to the farmers 'You can't plant so many coffee seedlings'. So they were just laughing at us, I think.[16]

Given that government officers did not control the actual distribution of seedlings, the only alternative would have been supervision of the selling by Agriculture officials. The Murang'a agricultural staff, however, was not large enough, as the foregoing quotation indicates. During the 1966 long rains, staff available to check on selling and planting of the infill quota consisted of the Cash Crops Officer, two agricultural assistants and, at necessarily irregular intervals, the DAO himself.[17] The DAO estimated that Departmental supervision, effected by unannounced visits to society nurseries and spot checks on receipt books, was 'about 20% of what was needed'.[18]

[15] Extracts from the report alleging that illegal planting had taken place were read to me by a government officer; I did not have sight of the document.
[16] Murang'a Agriculture Department official.
[17] DAO Murang'a (Mr D. B. Kahuthia) March 1967.
[18] Ibid.

The Murang'a Department of Agriculture took a tree census in October-November 1966,

> because we wanted to find out what had happened during the rains, and also we were getting ready, because the government was bringing in legislation to make it tougher for those farmers who did not want to follow the government on coffee. We were told by headquarters that we must see how well the restriction of 6% had worked, because there would be new regulations coming up to control planting, and also we would have Nairobi inspectors who could handle all this supervising because we did not have the staff....[19]

According to the results of the Department's census, over one million coffee trees had been planted during the long rains of a few months previously: in other words, Murang'a growers had planted more than three times the amount of coffee to which they were legally entitled. Moreover, according to officials, about half of the total number of seedlings were not planted as infills at all, but represented a further breach of the prohibition on new planting. (Some farmers had not bothered to attempt concealment of the fact that they were planting new coffee: when questioned by Departmental census-takers, they admitted that they had planted out fresh land, but argued that 'nobody' was abiding by the prohibition on new planting or the limitation on infilling in any case. Others, however, made some attempt to justify their planting in terms of the regulations. While they could not deny that new trees represented a greater proportion of their total trees than the permitted 6%, they argued that this was due to high losses from Coffee Berry Disease, and not to illegal new planting. In one case, a census-taker reported, a farmer had uprooted half a dozen mature trees and dotted them around a field of new planting, to lend wilting credence to his vain claim that he was 'infilling'.)

The Department's census results, showing that about one million trees had been planted in the rains, and further that Murang'a growers had about 24,000 acres under coffee instead of the authorized 20,661 acres, was challenged by the Union, speaking for its primary society members. Following a series of growers' meetings in November and December 1966, the secretary-manager of the Union, Geoffrey Kebatta, ordered that primary societies themselves should carry out a 'recount' of the number of trees on their members' holdings. This recount, the returns for which were collated by the Union by late January 1967, contended that only some 18-19,000 acres were under coffee. Further, the Union secretary-manager asserted that, since members were no longer allowed to plant infills to replace the full number of diseased or

[19] Ibid.

dead trees, there were actually only some 14,000 acres under live and healthy trees.[20] These assertions were based, according to the Union, on returns from the primary co-operative societies, and had been compiled from the registers drawn up under orders from the Ministry of Agriculture in Nairobi earlier in 1966. The Union sent a deputation to the Ministry in February 1967, led by Kebatta and the 'Union Patron', ex-senior chief Ndung'u Kagori, which made 'strong representations about the miscounting by (government) census-takers in the district'.[21]

The argument between the growers and the DAO about how much land was really under coffee had already by this time been subsumed in the new conflict over coffee planting provoked by the slashing of the infill allowance to 2% in January 1967. The figures of the Department and of the Union were plainly irreconcilable; and it is clear, from the admission of prominent growers that new planting prohibitions had not been observed since they were imposed in 1964, that the Union's figure of approximately 19,000 acres considerably underestimated the true position. If it were correct, it would mean that Murang'a coffee growers had not even seen fit to take up the coffee acreage allocated to them in 1964—a proposition which Kebatta admitted to be highly unlikely. The Union's figure, he said, might be a little on the low side because the registers were a recent innovation, and the primary societies had not yet got used to them nor had the opportunity to check them for accuracy.

Whatever the real coffee acreage, however, the rival estimates were in the main bargaining counters: Agriculture officials used the 24,000-acre census to justify stringent limitations on planting and the imminent arrival of coffee inspectors who, it was expected, would ruthlessly uproot illegal coffee and prosecute transgressors.[22] The growers, for their part, wished to establish that there was no 'control problem' in Murang'a, and that there was consequently no justification for prohibiting members of societies from at least replacing dead or diseased trees, even if national policy required that no new planting should be allowed. The growers were in something of a dilemma, however, because infill allowances were based in part on the registers, and low register totals meant low infill allocations.

But Murang'a growers' leaders regarded the dispute over acreage as a skirmish, rather than as the central struggle. Their main efforts were directed towards changing government policy on coffee control, at least as it affected Murang'a. In the months following the imposition of the 2% infill quota, therefore, arguments about the accuracy of tree and

[20] Geoffrey Kebatta, May 12th, 1967.
[21] Ibid.
[22] DAO's speech to management committee of Murang'a Farmers' Co-operative Union on January 14th, 1967. Summarized in Minute 341/67 of that meeting—fuller version supplied by Dept. of Agriculture, Murang'a.

acreage figures receded into the background: under the control conditions of 1967, the Murang'a leaders saw the conflict as being political, rather than as an argument with the local representatives of the Ministry of Agriculture about the implementation of government policy.

> You see my committee and all our growers felt it was necessary that it should be known what was the true position about coffee here in Murang'a. The Agriculture people were saying that we had far too much coffee planted in Murang'a ... but we knew that this would just be used against us. But also our members were concerned about this infill business, and in all those meetings which have been happening in Kandara and all over the district, they have been making it clear that they know that coffee is a very difficult thing to handle for the government, because of the Agreement ... but we felt that the government, right up to the President, must be aware of our feelings that Murang'a farmers are being very unfairly treated in this.[23]

The Department of Agriculture, it appears, was also having second thoughts about the census figures in January 1967, and subsequently. Although officers were in no doubt that the 1966 infill allowance had been substantially exceeded by Murang'a growers, they were prepared to admit, after the initial arguments with the growers, that their census might not be wholly accurate.

> The census figures were very late coming in and there was an even greater delay before these could be even partially checked with those of the Union, and so a full check on the accuracy of the census has not yet been possible. This is urgently required as there are slight indications that past estimates of the coffee acreage in Murang'a District were too high.[24]

Part of the reason for this more accommodating attitude lay in the fact that the Department had genuine doubts, and it was important to have good estimates for the successful implementation of coffee control policy. It was noted that accurate figures

> are essential for future policy of the planting of coffee in the district and on a local basis for the optimal siting of new coffee factories in 1967.[25]

---

[23] Interview with Samuel Karugu, chairman of the Union, April 21st, 1967.
[24] Murang'a District Annual Report for 1966, p. 21 (written end January 1967). The reference to 'past estimates' is to the figure of 23,161 acres as at November 30th, 1965, reproduced in Plan appendix, Table 11, p. 365.
[25] Ibid.

94 *Peasant Politics*

A further important factor, however, was political: officers were conscious that the coffee control policy was becoming the subject of political conflict, both between growers and Government (including its local agricultural representatives) and within the co-operative movement.

> Now last year, when all this trouble about the census was very bad, it got so bad that we could not even talk to the growers, except for just a few farmers who understood that we were only doing our job, and we were not responsible for what was decided in Nairobi. But most of them were going round at all these meetings saying that we were trying to kill off coffee here in Murang'a. Also some of them were trying to attack the Union, and were especially blaming Kebatta. But I think Mr Kathendu (the District Co-operative Officer) can say more about that. Anyway we felt that we must try to meet the farmers and agree with them what needed to be done, so we informed the Union that if we could agree on the census, it would be better for everyone ... because you see with the new infills coming up, and all these requirements for factories, the situation was very difficult for us.[26]

The Murang'a Department of Agriculture thus sought to minimize its role in the conflict. Officials impressed on their provincial superiors the need for avoiding conflict between the growers and government officers who, as well as being responsible for coffee control in the district, were also charged with the administration of agricultural policy in general.[27] The result, from the officers' viewpoint, was to make life considerably easier.

> The new coffee legislation, requiring each Society to keep an accurate record of the name and number of each grower and the number of trees he owns, will do this check automatically however, if implemented properly. The District is now awaiting the Coffee Inspectors to be appointed. Thus it has been decided by the Provincial Cash Crops Officer and the Senior Coffee Development Officer to leave the checking of the census to the Inspector.[28]

This decision was an important one for Murang'a Agriculture officials. It meant that in the ensuing conflict their role was of marginal importance: they had been effectively relieved of day-to-day responsibility for coffee control, and were therefore much less involved than

[26] Murang'a Agriculture official, February 27th, 1967.
[27] Agriculture official, February 1967.
[28] Department of Agriculture, Annual Report for 1966.

before in confrontations with the growers and their representatives.[29] The coffee inspector assigned to Murang'a was expected to have an easier task in controlling illegal coffee than Agriculture officials had had the previous year. He possessed the powers of summary uprooting conferred by the 1966 legislation and, more crucially, the government's policy of centralizing seedling nurseries would work decisively in his favour. With coffee growers denied access to seedlings at their individual society nurseries, it would be far easier to control illegal planting by keeping a close check on the central Union nursery. Coffee trees in primary society nurseries were to be uprooted during February and March (with compensation payable to the societies by the Coffee Board of Kenya at the rate of 20 cents each, a sum which would just cover nursery costs); subsequently, it was planned, the inspector would start to seek out illegally planted coffee and order it to be uprooted and, if the offence was sufficiently serious, start criminal proceedings against the grower.

As an essential preliminary, the DAO had gained the formal acceptance by the Union of the new centralized nursery arrangement. At its meeting on January 14th, the management committee passed the following resolution:

> In compliance with requirements of coffee planting restrictions, it is hereby agreed that all future supplies of coffee seedlings to coffee Co-operatives should be from Murang'a Farmers' Co-operative Union Ltd. nursery and that the Ministry of Agriculture and Coffee Board of Kenya should be requested to make all coffee seeds allocations for Murang'a District to Murang'a Farmers' Co-operative Union Ltd.[30]

Coffee growers' representatives had known for some time that seedlings were to be centralized in the Union nursery, and this had been accepted—albeit ungraciously—as inevitable. Some societies attempted to mitigate the effects of centralization by hastily selling off substantial quantities of seedlings before they were destroyed, and at least one society—Muruka Coffee Growers' Co-operative Society—sold its entire seedling stock to its members.[31]

But the prospect that illegal coffee belonging to individual growers was to be uprooted was far more serious—because the inspector defined illegal coffee *by reference to the registers* which the societies had been

---

[29] By April 1967, officers categorized their coffee control as 'advisory only'.
[30] Minute 341/67.
[31] The coffee inspector proposed to charge the Muruka committee with evading the 2% infill limitation, and with selling seedlings without issuing receipts. The papers were sent to the Attorney-General in April, but no charges were laid.

compelled to establish in 1966. Since the registers had been so compiled as to give artificially low figures, the amount of coffee which would now be defined as 'illegal' was correspondingly very high indeed.

The knowledge that the registers would be used against growers was undoubtedly a potent factor in mobilizing political resources against coffee control in the first half of 1967; it was, however, a catalyst rather than a root cause. As the foregoing narrative has indicated, Murang'a farmers had not been prepared to abide by planting restrictions when they were re-introduced in 1964; they had ignored the restrictions initially, and then manoeuvred to maintain maximum freedom from control when restrictions were tightened in 1966. Some of the techniques employed in the evasion of 1966 were now boomeranging, giving added impetus to the political battle against the policy. The new restrictions imposed at the beginning of 1967 made it impossible for coffee growers (or would-be growers) to expect to be able to avoid them any longer, and the alternatives were clearly seen by growers' leaders to be those of submitting to the new controls or bringing political pressure to bear on the government.

Kandara's Leadership

Although the main aim of the political campaign waged in 1967 was to end the infill restrictions and the uprooting of coffee, the restriction issue brought into focus other, related, grievances—over what the growers saw as discrimination in favour of the estates on the part of the Ministry of Agriculture, and over the levies and taxes extracted from growers by government and by the various components of the Kenyan coffee bureaucracy. As the Murang'a campaign gathered force, the attack was thus broadened into a general critique of alleged government unfairness to African growers—and especially to those in Murang'a.[32]

It is clear that the main impetus came initially from Kandara: a coffee inspector had not yet been appointed for Murang'a, and a Kiambu inspector therefore began work in Kandara division in mid-February. Some Kandara notables seemed to be as disturbed by the inspector's style as by what he was actually doing:

> Our members were telling us how this man was just coming from Thika and riding round the division. He was getting out of his car, and just looking round the *shambas*, and then riding away

---

[32] The issue of planting control was not the only concern of politicians and growers' leaders in this period: conflict within the co-operative movement, and efforts to prevent the implementation of co-operative reforms were also important. These issues are set out in the following chapter for the sake of clarity, although I am conscious that the division makes the discussion in this chapter somewhat superficial.

without saying anything. Some of our people were very upset.³³

Apart from the immediate crisis, however, Kandara coffee farmers had of course been active in the political arena for some time. They had formed an important core of support for the Atiriri Bururi Union in 1965, when Mwaura was engaged in his struggle with Kaggia for political primacy, and it was their influence, in large measure, which ensured that Ndirira voiced the pre-occupations of the wealthier farmers (and in particular the demands and grievances of the coffee farmers) as well as being Mwaura's personal political instrument.

The Kandara co-operative leaders and politicians were assisted in their campaign not only by this political tradition, but by the fact that Kandara coffee farmers, and to a lesser extent growers in the rest of the district, felt that they had been deprived of the opportunity to plant as much coffee as they would have wished owing to the re-consolidation carried out in Murang'a after 1960, which produced uncertainty over the ownership of land fragments—and hence of coffee trees—which inhibited wide-scale planting. This important factor will be more fully discussed below.

The Kandara coffee farmers who emerged in February-March 1967 as the prime movers in the campaign to change government policy included former leaders of the Ndirira campaigns. Prominent among them were ex-senior chief Ndung'u Kagori, who had led the deputation to Kenyatta in 1965 demanding Kaggia's dismissal from Parliament and from KANU. Ndung'u, now of advancing years, was said to have accumulated large landholdings while a colonial chief during the Emergency, and was certainly among the largest coffee growers in Kandara. During 1967 he held the title of 'Union Patron', having retired from the Union chairmanship the previous year. Ndung'u was recognized by Murang'a civil servants as a formidable political figure in Kandara.

> Chief Ndung'u is a very important man here. He has a lot of coffee, and he is also very influential among the co-operatives. I think it's because he has been powerful here a long time, that farmers will always listen to him, and they always send him with these delegations to see *Mzee,* because even *Mzee* listens to him ...³⁴

The Kandara group, led by Ndung'u and by Jasmel Kariuki, also an ex-Ndirira man and vice-chairman of the Union, included another ex-chief, Erastus Kigera (chairman of Nginda Society), Ndung'u's son Francis Ndung'u (a Union delegate from Gacharage Society), Godfrey

---
³³ Jasmel Kariuki, May 27th, 1967.
³⁴ Administration Officer, March 24th, 1967.

Waweru (chairman of Kagunduini Society), and yet another chief—this time a serving one: Peter Kimemia, chairman of Gacharage Society and a bitter opponent of Kaggia during the political conflict in the division in 1964 and 1965.

Initally, then, the political fight against coffee restrictions was led by a powerful section of the Murang'a co-operative leadership, represented by men with long-standing and influential connections with Kandara KANU leaders, and with political influence—at least in the case of Ndung'u Kagori and Kigera—extending outside the division and the district up to the President himself. They were, in effect, the agricultural section of the dominant conservative alliance in Kandara politics—an alliance which, as was suggested in Chapter 3, consisted of former Home Guard and loyalist elements and of rural traders and entrepreneurs, and which drew its mass support from the small farmers who felt that the ethic of *Harambee* and individualism offered them scope for personal advancement. The combination of peasant leaders, and newer commercial petty bourgeoisie had been assured of political primacy since Kaggia's defeat in 1966, but the coffee planting restrictions were seen as being of the same order of importance as Kaggia's political threat had been: less fundamental, perhaps, but touching their incomes much more directly.

> We feel very seriously that the government must not act hastily over this coffee matter, because Murang'a is nothing if you take away coffee. . . . This division was nearly led astray in earlier times by Kaggia and his few supporters, but we were always supporters of the true KANU, and we feel that soon there will be nothing left if the government does not listen to us.[35]

Kandara alone accounted for almost half the total coffee acreage in Murang'a (insofar as this can be estimated); the combination of vital economic interest and a volatile political tradition made the division's leadership of the struggle against restrictions almost inevitable. Indeed, even before the campaign was properly under way, administrators were wearily predicting 'plenty of trouble' from the area over the new infill policy.

Mwaura, Thabuni and other Kandara KANU leaders began holding 'KANU growers' meetings' in the division from mid-February, at which resolutions were passed condemning the infill restrictions and the proposed uprooting of illegal coffee, and urging the government to rescind the new control policy. At the same time, Kandara delegates to the Union management committee were foremost in urging that the Union should refuse to co-operate in the centralization of the seedling supply[36]—despite the unanimous resolution which had agreed to

---

[35] Jasmel Karuiki, May 20th, 1967.
[36] Kebatta, May 12th, 1967.

comply with this aspect of government policy. The campaign in Kandara elicited a strong response from growers from the beginning, not least because the coffee inspector, working from Thika, was already a tangible presence in the division. It took some time for political activity on a comparable scale to develop in the other divisions, however: in part, this reflected the tensions between Kandara KANU leaders and the followers of Kiano in the other divisions. But while it was only with difficulty that Kandara leaders could extend their campaigns within the party outside the division, within the co-operative movement Ndung'u Kagori and his allies recruited non-Kandara supporters more quickly. Thus KANU in Kandara was intimately associated with the campaign from the beginning, but in the other divisions the party became actively involved only at a later stage— sometime early in April, it seems—when uprooting had already begun and growers throughout the district were demanding action from their political representatives.

> I think there was a feeling that KANU should not try to embarrass the government, and they more or less tried to stay out of things at first. . . . The Kandara people eventually changed that, but in any case the growers are very important in KANU, so they had to become involved.[37]

Jasmel Kariuki, Mwangi Thabuni and another Kandara member of the County Council, Samuel Gachau (also an ex-chief and an associate of Ndung'u Kagori) sponsored an anti-uprooting resolution at a meeting of the County Council on April 6th. In the debate, Kandara members said that a large number of Kandara and Makuyu farmers had been informed that they would have to uproot coffee planted in 1966, and that the coffee inspector had already supervised the uprooting of a substantial amount of coffee. (Thabuni subsequently asserted that 143 farmers had been served with notices demanding some uprooting, and that a further 40 had already had some trees grubbed up. These statements could not be verified, since neither the Department of Agriculture nor the Coffee Board of Kenya could, or would give details of the number of farmers or the number of trees involved. It seems, however, that the first concern of the inspector had been to reduce the number of trees illegally planted during the 1966 long rains, and he was therefore demanding that a proportion of the youngest seedlings on each *shamba* inspected be uprooted.) The Council resolved that no trees planted in 1966 should be uprooted, and that where uprooting had already taken place the farmers concerned should be compensated by government.

The Council meeting was the first public sign that the campaign against restrictions was gathering wide support from KANU leaders

---

[37] Agriculture Department official, August 1967.

outside Kandara. Although the non-Kandara MPs—Kiano, Gachago and Njiiri—had not allowed themselves to be publicly associated with the anti-restriction lobby (all three were, after all, members of the Government), their supporters were now prepared to join the Kandara group in vigorous opposition. KANU leaders in Kigumo, Kiharu and Kangema called special meetings of coffee growers during April to discuss action against infill restrictions, and met with primary society committees, where the latter were amenable, or with individual members who were also active in the party.[38] The agitation was given an added urgency with the Ministry of Agriculture's announcement on May 2nd that the Minister had ordered that *all* Union, primary society and commercial nursery seedlings surplus to the 2% allowance were to be destroyed by coffee inspectors and the owners compensated at 20 cents per seedling. Although it had earlier been known that this was to be done, the Minister's announcement, with its implication of immediate action, helped to consolidate support for the political campaign being waged by KANU and the Kandara growers. The Ministry's instructions, transmitted to the Union and to the primary societies through the Agricultural Officer, advised the societies to do the uprooting themselves, rather than await action by the coffee inspector. Needless to say, none of the societies intended to follow this advice; furthermore, committee members were genuinely confused as to how surpluses were to be assessed. With the confusion over the Government census and the Union's figures, and with primary society registers still not reliable as a guide to acreages, the management committees asked 'Two per cent of what?'[39]

KANU's activity culminated in a meeting, attended by party leaders and a large number of primary society committee members, in the Murang'a County Council chamber on May 6th. The meeting was called to discuss 'co-operative developments within the district' rather than the question of planting restrictions, but much debate of course concentrated on combatting the threat to coffee growers. As the following chapter will make clear, however, the KANU leadership was by no means simply concerned with supporting the growers' case against coffee control: while the infill restrictions were condemned and the demand made that society nurseries should be maintained, the meeting had at least as much significance for local politics and in particular for the political conflicts within the co-operative movement as it did for the campaign against control. In the context of this chapter, however, the importance of the meeting lay in the fact that the KANU leadership was now unequivocally associated with the growers in fighting controls, and secondly in the fact that the Union, under

[38] District Co-operative Officer and Kebatta.
[39] Kebatta, May 20th, 1967.

pressure both from the politicians and from the Kandara co-operative leaders (both of whom were trying to assign some blame for restrictions to the Union) was compelled to seek an accommodation with the political leaders which would both advance the growers' cause and protect the Union from further attacks by politicians.

The May 6th conference also provided a stimulus for the Administration, which had till then apparently not been actively involved in the controversy. Even now, the District Commissioner's concern was not so much the planting control issue as the struggle within the co-operative movement in Murang'a: it was the DC's office which suggested to the Union that a meeting should be held to which KANU functionaries should be invited, to patch up the conflict between the two organizations.

> I think the Administration here was concerned about this situation, and they thought we ought to get together to try and solve it. . . . In fact the Chairman (of the Union) had already said to me that we would have to do something like this, but then it was more urgent when the DC wanted to come and speak to the delegates.[40]

A special general meeting of the Union was called for May 20th, and was held in the Union's board room. Aside from the chairmen of the primary societies (i.e. the usual members of the Union management committee) 64 other delegates attended from the co-operatives, as did 20 KANU leaders. The KANU delegation was led by the two MPs from Kandara, Mwaura and Wanjagi, the Chairman of the County Council, Kamau Njoroge and his Vice-Chairman, and four other councillors—three of them, from Kangema, effectively representing Kiano.[41] Among the other members of the KANU delegation were four local KANU chairmen—all from Kandara—and Ndaba Karomo, the Kandara member of the Provincial Advisory Council. The activism of the Kandara politicians was thus once more in evidence: not only was the KANU delegation decisively weighted in their favour, but the Kandara primary society delegates, who stood in a block near the platform, were more active participants in discussion and in putting resolutions than delegates from other societies.

This is not to suggest that the other divisions were being carried unwillingly along; as the earlier narrative has suggested, the proselytizing of the Kandara group in the preceding weeks had induced an activism in the other societies that had not been evident before. The role of Ndung'u Kagori and his associates, by their politicization of the

[40] Kebatta, June 23rd, 1967.
[41] One of them, Kabiri Mahugu, stated that the Kangema councillors were 'representing the politicians of our division'.

planting control issue, had been to provide a platform for collective grower protest against government policy where before only the Union had fulfilled that function—and then not to the growers' satisfaction.

The Growers' Demands

The special meeting of May 20th was the Union's response both to the need to reassert itself as the legitimate voice of Murang'a coffee growers and to the internal crisis within the co-operative movement. The outcome of the meeting as it affected coffee control policy was clear. It was unanimously resolved:

> 2% coffee seedling infills are unfair treatment to small African growers who are mainly the coffee Co-operatives and should therefore be reviewed to allow all misses and gaps in authorized acreage of a district; and as such coffee seedlings in Co-operative nurseries should not be uprooted for destruction.
>
> Government be and is hereby urged to order uprooting of old plantation coffee in lower areas and/or appoint a commission to investigate into and formulate possibilities of reducing large coffee acreage plantations owned by individuals with a view of enabling small African coffee growers to plant an economic unit of coffee acreage within Co-operatives.[42]

These were the most radical demands yet put forward by Murang'a growers. Although opposition to the 2% restriction had been clear from the beginning growers' leaders had not up to this point defined what restrictions *would* be acceptable. The meeting made clear that they wanted the abolition of *all* infill restrictions—in other words, a return to the situation which had existed immediately after the prohibition on *new* planting in 1964. The growers had learnt between 1964 and 1967 that the rub could be taken out of new planting restrictions by the primary societies having control over their own nurseries; the demand that primary society nurseries should retain their seedlings underlined the fact that access to seedlings was the crucial factor in coffee control.

The second resolution took the growers into even wider issues of public policy—issues on which the government clearly felt vulnerable. The economic dominance of the settler community had of course for long been the central issue in Kenyan politics, and after independence European control of critical economic resources remained contentious, because its reality contradicted the autonomy which formal independence had been supposed to secure. The issue was not solely of transferring control to African hands, although the importance the government attached to black capitalist participation is clear. In

[42] Minute 4.

Parliament and elsewhere, politicians had also been concerned with other questions, such as the burdensome terms on which transfer of the White Highlands to Africans under the Million Acre Scheme was taking place, and the disadvantages which African farmers and entrepreneurs were felt to suffer in particular areas or commodities. Whether the issue was the general one of European hegemony over the economy, or its implications in particular instances, the government had, since independence, been faced with a fairly persistent critique of its policies—by no means always from an identifiable 'leftist' wing within KANU, nor later exclusively from the KPU. Thus where the government sought African control of commerce and industry by Africanizing managerial positions within European-dominated enterprises and, where possible, by partnership between African and neo-colonial capital, its parliamentary critics called for nationalization of major commercial enterprises and industries. On land, the government maintained that transfers should be on a willing buyer-willing seller basis, and that it was bound by the independence package deal on British finance for buying out white farmers; a substantial number of MPs wanted more land transferred more quickly, and were incensed that settlers should be receiving such high prices for their farms.

It is in this sense that the Murang'a growers were 'radical': they were proposing a far more drastic solution to the squeeze on African coffee growers than government had hitherto been willing to accept. As the growers saw it, the government was in effect discriminating against them by treating estates and co-operatives alike—it was freezing an inequitable situation.

> The Europeans have had all these years when Africans were not permitted to grow coffee, and so they have these very big plantations full of coffee, and it is only quite recently that Africans could grow a few small acres of coffee. But now everybody must stop, and all those settlers are quite all right.[43]

The government had attempted in 1966 to redress the balance—although only slightly—in favour of African growers by setting up the Coffee Authority, designed to help rationalize production in the co-operatives, notably by giving loans to societies for the construction of coffee factories. In Murang'a, growers regarded the Authority not as a minor blessing but as a further discrimination: it was yet another financial burden on growers, another addition to the coffee bureaucracy which growers felt was already too big and too expensive. Aside from their primary societies and the Union, Murang'a growers, like all Kenyan African growers, helped support four separate bodies. The

[43] Kebatta, May 12th, 1967.

Kenya Planters' Co-operative Union fulfilled two important functions—it owned the mills in which all Kenyan coffee was milled, and it acted as wholesale purchasing agency for coffee growers' supplies, charging a ¼% levy for this service. The Coffee Board of Kenya a statutory authority, acted as government agent in the control of the coffee industry, licensing growers and nurseries, and authorizing the supply of seed from the Coffee Research Foundation at Ruiru in Kiambu. From 1967 it was the Board which employed the coffee inspectors to discharge its control functions. The Coffee Marketing Board's function was to purchase the whole of the coffee crop for resale at the best available prices: like the CBK and the Coffee Authority, its administrative and other costs were borne by the growers, to the tune of £1½ million in 1966.[44] The justness of criticism of this structure was implicitly recognized in a rationalization of the institutions shortly after this period.

The cost to coffee growers of the new Authority was projected, soon after its establishment, at a mere £120,000 a year; but it was not primarily on financial grounds (which were not very strong, in view of this modest sum) that its establishment aroused such acute hostility in Murang'a. It excited opposition as a symbol of discrimination, and as what was seen as yet another opportunity for patronage in Nairobi, with the farmer bearing the cost. The growers' arguments against the large structure administering the production and marketing of Kenya coffee were not specific: they rested on a conviction that farmers were being fleeced with little apparent benefit to themselves (hardly an uncommon rural sentiment). Disgruntlement at the levies which these bodies exacted on growers' proceeds had been given political significance, however, by the severe restrictions on planting (administered by the Coffee Board) and by the fact that the newest accretion was the outcome of a political decision on a profoundly important issue: *the establishment of the Coffee Authority was, and was seen to be, a decision against the reduction of European-owned coffee acreages to make more room for Africans to grow coffee within the quota*. Thus the only avenue offered to African growers was to improve the quality of their coffee, mainly by expanding processing facilities with the aid of Coffee Authority loans, funded by the African growers themselves.

The Union's management committee had resolved at its meeting on April 21st that it was strongly opposed to the existence of the Authority in its present form, and objected to any co-operative money being spent in the Authority's operations. It appointed a delegation to the Minister for Co-operatives to press its viewpoint, but the more pressing events of the ensuing weeks meant that no visit took place. An

[44] Parliamentary Report, December 1st, 1966, col. 2244.

even more forthright resolution was passed at the special meeting between the Union and KANU leaders on May 20th:

> Coffee Authority, being an organization established for African coffee Co-operatives only, and not affecting coffee plantations which are mainly owned by wealthy non-Africans, should be abolished and the government is hereby urged to abolish it forthwith to save African peasant coffee growers from unscrupulous exploitations.
>
> Coffee industry statutory boards should be reduced, and Government is hereby urged to reduce them to the minimum of economic requirement with a view to saving growers from unnecessary expenses.

Again, the issue was not simply one of grower resentment against the statutory boards and the expense of maintaining them. Particularly in the case of the KANU leaders and the moving spirits among the Kandara growers, there was little desire to differentiate between the public authorities involved and the Union—indeed, many of the attacks on the Union discussed in the following chapter associated the Union, in terms of expense and responsibility for growers' grievances, with the statutory boards. In addition, part of the resentment against the CBK and the Coffee Authority involved funding, control and repayment arrangements for coffee factory loans to Murang'a primary societies, and once again reflected the tensions and conflicts in the co-operative movement and in Murang'a politics.

The Growers' Victory

Nevertheless, Murang'a growers' leaders and KANU politicians had papered over local differences sufficiently to present a series of unanimously supported demands to government on the three most pressing issues: infill restrictions, the European estates and the control bodies. The May 20th meeting also resolved that a delegation should be appointed 'to present and discuss these resolutions to the Minister of Agriculture and Animal Husbandry and further presentation to the Government'. It is interesting that this delegation was not chosen at the meeting as previous ones had been; as it never went to Nairobi, perhaps it was never intended to, but was more of a show of determination to back up informal contacts by those Murang'a leaders who had personal access to the President.

It is clear that urgent representations were made to the government by Murang'a politicians. Whether Murang'a notables had visited the President to discuss the coffee issue before the May 20th meeting was not clear, although in any event the government could hardly have been unaware of the demands of the district's growers. Certainly after the meeting co-operative leaders were in no doubt that pressure would be exerted on the President: Kebatta said that the issue 'is now out of our hands—it goes right up into national politics and there is nothing more we can do'. The Union chairman, Samuel Karugu, was more specific:

> I think the Murang'a people have now made their voice clear, and our President will have to listen. Murang'a leaders can have a lot to say to *Mzee* if they want to, and I think *Mzee* will listen to Gikonyo (Kiano) and Ndung'u (Kagori) if they go to see him.[45]

Five days after the special meeting of the Union, it was announced that a 'KANU leaders' conference' would be held on May 28th, in three days' time, to be followed by a rally at Fort Hall Stadium.[46] This was the venue chosen to announce the President's decision that all uprooting of coffee in African areas was to stop immediately. James Gichuru, Minister of Finance and acting Minister of Agriculture in Bruce McKenzie's absence from the country, told the KANU rally as earlier he had told the KANU leaders that coffee inspectors would stop work immediately. They would, however, continue to uproot illegal or neglected coffee on the European estates.

The Government's choice of the KANU conference in Murang'a as the occasion on which to announce the President's decision was a clear indication that Murang'a was recognized to be the centre of resistance. There had been complaints about the control policies from the other districts, but none appears to have been so determined in its opposition as Murang'a. To some extent, Murang'a's predominance stemmed from the fact that the struggle of the district's growers' leaders against restriction, and particularly the later political character of that struggle, involved local issues: Kandara committee men, and Kandara KANU leaders in particular, used grower resentment against planting control in their attempts to subvert the authority of the Union and of the Co-operative Officer within the Murang'a co-operative movement.

But a more important reason is hinted at in the annual report for 1967 of the Coffee Board of Kenya:

> There is little doubt that this order (that uprooting of African coffee should stop) was issued on misrepresentations emanating particularly from a certain area which was anxious to continue planting coffee.

The desire to continue planting coffee in Murang'a did not stem simply

---

[45] Karugu, May 20th, 1967.
[46] Hand-written notices were posted at Administration headquarters, Fort Hall, at District Officers' offices in the divisions, and some were also displayed at local markets and chiefs' camps.

from the fact that coffee was a lucrative crop for peasant farmers; the critical factor was that Murang'a coffee farmers (and also farmers who had not planted any coffee at all before new planting was banned in 1964) clearly felt that they had been prevented from taking full advantage of the opportunity that coffee growing presented to African farmers in the early Sixties. This sense of deprivation was expressed in conversations with many growers, and the reasons for it were aptly summarized by Kamau Njoroge:

> You see Murang'a should really have the most coffee in Kenya—even double what we have got, because the district is very suitable for it. What has happened here is due to the mix-up with land consolidation.... When they said that consolidation was going to be done all over again here in the district, it put us seriously behind, because (in the early Sixties) all the other districts were planting a lot of coffee, but here it was no good to plant coffee on your *shamba,* because the next day they gather up the fragments (of land), and then the DO says no, your coffee belongs to someone else, because now your land has been consolidated with his farm, and you have got this other piece over here . . .[47]

It is, of course, impossible to say how big an effect this factor had on Murang'a during the 1963-64 planting rush, when African farmers could put as many acres under coffee as they wished after the breakdown of Agriculture Department controls. Very substantial acreages were of course planted throughout the district, but there is little doubt that, particularly in Kandara, where even the new consolidation ran into opposition and considerable delay, many farmers held back from planting coffee on their fragments, for fear of losing it when consolidation was completed. (An echo of the old consolidation battles of 1963-65 could be heard in a KANU anti-Kaggia poster which appeared in the district in June 1967, which accused Kaggia, inter alia, of preventing farmers from planting coffee—a reference to Kaggia's activities over consolidation, and his advice to Kandara farmers not to plant land with long-term crops where they could not be sure of retaining ownership when consolidation was properly carried out.) By the time the re-consolidation was nearing completion, new planting had been banned and, despite widespread evasion of the prohibition, many farmers could not plant coffee at all, or had much smaller numbers of trees than they would have wished. Murang'a politicians consequently had greater reason to combat the restrictions than had leaders in other districts. The CBK was not in any doubt that Murang'a was responsible for the President's decision to stop the uprooting; nor were the

[47] July 1967.

district's politicians and co-operative leaders. Just how that decision was reached, and how pressure was brought to bear by district leaders (obviously supported, although with less vehemence, by other coffee-growing districts) was impossible to discover. What is clear, however, is that the order was made by the President himself, and not by the Cabinet or the Minister of Agriculture: if it had been a collective or departmental decision, there would surely have been little likelihood of the confusion which followed Gichuru's bare statement that uprooting of African coffee would be stopped.

In practice, of course, stopping the uprooting meant abandoning the 2% infill restriction, since coffee inspectors were now not permitted to destroy the illegal coffee of individual growers and primary society nurseries were now assured of the safety of their seedlings, the Ministry of Agriculture's announcement of May 2nd notwithstanding. A few days after the Fort Hall rally, however, the Ministry stated that 'action would be taken' against those who planted coffee illegally[48]—precisely what form of action was not specified. Two days later, it was reported that the Assistant Minister of Agriculture had said that the President's intervention applied, not to individual growers' illegal trees, but only to primary society nursery seedlings.[49] Gichuru had made no such qualification: moreover, individual growers in Gatundu, the President's home area, who had had trees uprooted and fines imposed on them for growing illegal coffee, were in the weeks following *Mzee's* announcement compensated for their lost trees, and had their fines returned! The Department of Agriculture had thus been caught off balance by the President making a political decision, because of unrest in coffee areas and in Murang'a in particular, without reference to or prior consultation with the Department most concerned. The importance of that decision was emphasized by the Board and the Minister of Agriculture finally conceding defeat in September 1967.

> The Board again advised the Minister that it would be unable to control the illegal issue of seedlings from society nurseries and the Minister agreed to allow society nurseries to be run down for infilling purposes only, *irrespective of the 2%*[50]

Murang'a political leaders were thus able to effect a decisive change in the government's development policy. The economic and social effects of their defeat of control measures have not been clear, however: if the assessment of Kenya's coffee production problems presented by the government was right, the effects of the failure of control might have

---

[48] Ministry of Agriculture press statement, reported in *East African Standard,* June 5th, 1967.
[49] *Daily Nation,* June 7th, 1967.
[50] Coffee Board of Kenya *Annual Report* for 1967.

been expected to be severe indeed from about 1970 onward, as the freely planted 'illegal' trees came into bearing. At that stage, the problems of tight ICA quotas and chronic overproduction would have been accentuated by a 'production bulge' from the wholesale planting out of primary society seedlings (although it is possible that there would have been a *continued* upward trend rather than a 'bulge', if pre-1967 controls were evaded in other districts as widely as they were in Murang'a), forcing upon growers and government alike a new set of political choices.

This had not been the case, however: Kenya coffee production was seriously affected by Coffee Berry Disease and, during the latter half of 1967, by extended rain which aided the spread of the disease. Weather and disease thus helped to accomplish what government could not. Production dropped by nearly 9,000 tons in 1967 and by a further 8,000-odd in 1968, making the total production of 39,600 tons in 1968 some 30% below the 1966 figure.[51] And in addition to the bearing trees killed, of course, a fair proportion of immature trees must also have suffered. Adverse internal conditions, and the world production difficulties alluded to at the start of this chapter, thus allowed much-needed breathing space for the government, allowing it to plan once more for expansion. Aside from the relaxed quotas resulting from underproduction, however, the 1969 Development Plan also took account of marketing possibilities in non-quota countries, and in this new approach, so firmly resisted in 1967 and before, the government's awareness of the political problems of production control can have played no small part.

The defeat of planting control was not the only success over central government scored by the district's political leadership: government initiatives for the reform of the co-operative movement were also rendered ineffective in a number of important respects, as the following chapter will show. Unlike the battle over planting, however, this one was fought out entirely at the local level, within KANU and the local co-operative movement. Both conflicts reflected the capacity of district politicians to modify development policy, and the actors and arenas were for the most part the same, so that any attempt to draw general conclusions from either is therefore best left until both have been described.

---

[51] Standard Bank *Annual Economic Reviews* of Kenya, 1968 and 1969. Despite a considerable measure of recovery, in fact, exports to quota markets for the crop season 1968/9 were below Kenya's I.C.A. quota for the third year running; therefore, under the penalty rules, the country's quota was cut by 5,000 tons to 47,555 metric tons for 1969/70.

Chapter VI

COFFEE, CO-OPERATIVES AND POLITICS

The intense political activity among Murang'a coffee growers in the first half of 1967 contained a number of important elements, of which the conflict over coffee planting described in the previous chapter was only one. The effort of Murang'a growers and their representatives to modify or nullify government restrictions is of obvious importance to an analysis of the process of rural development and the Kenyan government's agricultural development policy: it emphasizes, above all, that agricultural development is multi-dimensional, involving not only the familiar problems of inducing peasants to grow cash crops or adopt improved productive methods instead of sticking to 'traditional' ways, but also of preventing peasant farmers from continuing to do something 'modern' and making them do something else instead. The traditional/modern dichotomy thus does not explain the economic and political choices involved, at least where, as in Murang'a, the nature of rural production could no longer be called 'traditional', in spite of a considerable subsistence sector. There had already been a substantial infusion of modern crops and agricultural techniques, drastic changes in social structure and land tenure, and some diversification into non-agricultural forms of economic activity.

The choices before Murang'a coffee growers were thus more complex and more subtle, involving the growers' evaluation of government agricultural strategy (and particularly its *de facto* pro-estate bias) and of the political and economic risks of non-compliance with government policy. The former is relevant to any discussion of parochial consciousness or localized 'moral horizons'; the latter assessment throws light on the nature of Kikuyu politics and the political relationships between district and centre—in other words on the structural rather than the cognitive or ideological aspects of local-central politics, to adopt for the moment a rather artificial distinction.

But the form which the Murang'a campaign against planting control took was to a significant degree determined by the dispositions of power within the district's co-operative movement, and by the activities of politicians from outside the movement seeking allies (or being sought as allies) and pursuing political goals within it. The struggle against planting restrictions provided the theme in 1967 for internal political conflicts which had been going on for some time, and which were given added impetus by the restrictions and by attempts at co-operative reform. The reform measures were seen by Government as being complementary to its strategy for coffee control, as the quotation from the Development Plan at page 87 above makes clear. As Ronald Ngala, the Minister for Co-operative and Social Services, said in opening the debate on the second reading of the 1966 Co-operative Societies Bill, the reasons for bringing about co-operative reform centred on the need for better control over the management, organization and finance of the movement. He added that lack of control had produced a major evil—misappropriation of society funds—which reform was also designed to prevent, and quoted the case of one society which had lost £35,000 in repeated frauds since independence.[1] He continued, in a passage of particular relevance to Murang'a:

> Although the Bill does not cover the aspect which would emphasize politics, I would like to make it quite clear that co-operative societies should be left free from political interference because where you have political interference, committee members tend to gang up probably to oust the person who has the bigger share in the co-operative society, or probably to oust a political opponent who is also a member of a co-operative committee. This brings about a lot of confusion and hostility in the committees of co-operative societies. I would like, therefore, to urge members and the country that it is very important that the co-operative movement should be entirely free from politics. It is also hoped that political leaders will encourage in practical terms so that we do not, either at the local level of politics or at the national level of politics, get involved in unnecessary politics in the co-operative movement.[2]

The co-operative movement in Murang'a exhibited many of the ills which the reform measures were designed to cure, as will become clear. But Murang'a co-operatives also demonstrated that the problem to be tackled had enduring roots, not readily susceptible to legal and administrative reform, in the social and political context within which the co-operatives operated.

[1] Parliamentary Reports, November 30th, 1966, col. 2182.
[2] Ibid. col. 2186/7.

The Attempt to Enforce Reform

The 'politicization' of co-operative affairs was a gradual process, which apparently accelerated with the settlement of the KANU branch's leadership dispute in 1966. In Chapter 3 it was intimated that the settlement by Party Headquarters in favour of Kiano was the immediate cause of increased interest by politicians in co-operative affairs; certainly Administrative officers attested to increased 'meddling' in society affairs by KANU politicians in the latter part of 1966, and in Kandara it seems that there was a marked increase during that period in the influence of such men as Ndung'u Kagori and Jasmel Kariuki, who had close connections with the Mwaura group. In the case of Kandara particularly, however, it is arguable that the political alliances between politicians and committee members which became apparent during 1966 and which assumed such importance during the following year were based on perceived class interests, and did not stem directly from the leadership contest being settled: the Mwaura group was seen in Kandara as representing the wealthier farmers and traders. This was particularly true after Mwaura's victory in the Little General Election, when distinctions of social class and ideology became even more apparent than they had earlier been. The interest which local politicians had in becoming increasingly involved in co-operative affairs will emerge more clearly in the course of this chapter; for the co-operative leaders' part, however, their motives in seeking political allies were clear enough. From later 1966 they were faced with government initiatives on two issues vital to their interest—drastic restrictions on coffee planting, and the imposition of stringent control over internal co-operative affairs. On the first issue, their interest in opposing government policy was identical with that of the growers they represented; the same is not true of co-operative reform, for the laxity and inefficiency of many primary societies conferred substantial financial benefits on the more astute committee members.

The co-operative reforms certainly increased the government's powers of control over the movement, and were clearly intended to ensure that it would act in concert with government's agricultural development policy. The administrative arrangements designed to implement this control, however, fell considerably short of direct control over the affairs of each primary society: as the Rules indicate, the main responsibility, at least in day-to-day terms, fell on the district co-operative unions.

> It is Government policy to encourage the formation of district co-operative unions, each union covering a geographical area (which may be the same as or smaller than an administrative district) whose primary societies, all crops being included, have a

turnover approaching £500,000 or more. Some 25 unions have already been formed, some of them operating on a mono-crop basis. The unions carry overall responsibility for the development and operations of primary societies in their areas. Theoretically it is their function to: provide transportation, marketing, accounting and other administrative services; determine terms of service of society staff members and arrange their recruitment and training; and make recommendations to the Commissioner on new applications for registration. The draft Co-operative Societies Act gives district unions power similar to those of the Commissioner, subject to his overall co-ordination and direction. It is the Government's aim to build up unions to the point *where it can rely on them* to keep the primary societies on a sound footing and generally *implement Government policies at the primary level.*[3]

With the passing of the Co-operative Societies Act and the publication of the Rules, therefore, the Murang'a Farmers' Co-operative Union underwent an important functional change. Since its formation in August 1960 it had been the central organization of Murang'a coffee farmers: it had provided administrative and technical services where primary societies chose to make use of them, operated as the medium through which the crop was marketed and payments made, and had been the authoritative voice of the growers in such forums as the Coffee Board of Kenya and the annual Coffee Conference. From late 1966, however, it became a hybrid organization: while continuing to represent the interests of its members, the primary societies, it now had clearly defined functions as an agent of the Commissioner for Co-operative Development.

Manpower shortages undoubtedly played an important part in the government's decision to transfer these functions to the unions. Even after the reforms were implemented, the government anticipated, the Department of Co-operatives would remain heavily dependent on American and Scandinavian assistance. It would be some time before the expanded training programme could have a significant effect in the field.[4] Co-operative Department officers in the field—perhaps three of four per district—could not cope with a new workload of such magnitude, whereas the unions already possessed specialized staff, close communications with the primary societies, and their own financial resources. At the same time, there is a more general rationale implicit in the ideology of Kenyan planning. Kenyan planning strategy sought to identify the minimum number of critical points at which government

[3] Development Plan, p. 201 (my emphasis).
[4] Ibid. p. 201, 202.

control had to be established to ensure the achievement of stated planning goals, while leaving most economic activity in private hands.

The government's initiative on co-operative reform, establishing a framework of controls by refraining in the main from direct enforcement, was in accordance with this general approach. The effects of the new reforms in Murang'a were varied: the new legal measures did not have the desired effect, but their existence and the efforts of government officers and union officials to implement them stimulated conflicts within the movement between the 'legalists' and 'reformers' on the one hand and those whose interests they threatened on the other.

On January 10th, 1967 the Co-operative Officer circulated a copy of the Rules to the secretary-manager of each Murang'a primary society, with a covering letter:

> 1. Despite the fact that new Co-operative Rules require all orders to be channelled through the Union, it has come to my notice that some societies are making orders contrary to Rule 4(v) of the Act, as shown in Legal Notice no. 189 . . .
>
> 2. It has also been realized that some societies are taking advices on coffee matters from some people—such as salesmen from some commercial companies. Any advice regarding coffee machinery etc. should be found from the Department of Agriculture.
>
> 3. This is now to remind you that all society orders should be made to or through the Murang'a Farmers' Co-operative Union in which your society is a member. No orders shall be valid which are made contrary to these Rules—any officer of the society who may not comply with these Rules could be held personally responsible, and may be surcharged as outlined in section 77(1) of the Co-operative Societies Act . . .

The Rules and the letter were accompanied by a note from Kebatta addressed to the secretary-managers and chairmen of all primary societies in the district.

> Please have the above Co-operative Societies Rules read, explained to your Society Management Committee and noted. These are in conformity with the reorganization now going on in this Union for Co-operative Societies for this District; which your Society has, in accordance with these Rules, to comply with.

These documents embody the primary economic causes of the developing conflict within the co-operative movement. The Co-operative Officer had identified the sections of the Rules which caused most hostility from the more vocal primary society committee members, and Kebatta's demand for compliance unequivocally associated the Union with the implementation of the Rules.

The ordering of supplies—fertilizer, coffee machinery, office equipment, building materials—had long offered committee members the opportunity for substantial financial gains.[5] Kenyan co-operative leaders and employees had in the past perpetrated fairly crude frauds with society funds, as the Development Plan had noted: absconding with large sums of money, or simply drawing money for goods which were never ordered. The incidence of these grosser forms of misappropriation had declined, in Murang'a at least, during 1966, with the conviction of a few offenders and a general tightening of official supervision in preparation for the forthcoming reforms. In particular, government officers made determined efforts to ensure that society accounts were prepared more quickly and audited more closely, thereby increasing the speed and likelihood of discovering fraud. With these administrative pressures, and the foreknowledge that even more stringent control was soon to be introduced, there had evolved more sophisticated operations to ensure that committee members' proceeds of office were maintained—of which the 'personal discount' system was the most widespread. A primary society committee would place an order for fertilizer, for example, with an Asian wholesaler in Thika, at a price substantially above that quoted by the Union. The primary society would pay the inflated price, but the members of the committee would be paid a 'personal discount' (i.e. a kickback) amounting to anything between 5% and 25% of the price, depending on the value of the order.

The existence of this system is of course not easily susceptible to documentary proof. However, aside from the fact that many co-operative leaders accepted that it did exist (although naturally not in their own societies), both Kebatta and the Co-operative Officer produced tender documents and primary societies' invoices as strong circumstantial evidence. One set of documents showed, for example, that a number of Kandara societies were regularly buying A.S.N. fertilizer from a Thika trader at Shs. 65/- per bag, when the Union offered the same fertilizer (supplied under tender through the Kenya Planters' Co-operative Union by Dalgety's East Africa) at Shs. 51/50.

The societies in which these and similar activities seem to have been most common were all in Kandara: it is almost certain that other committees were doing the same thing, but clearly not with the same frequency or determination. According to Kebatta,

It's really the Kandara people who give the most trouble with this

---

[5] I have avoided specific allegations in the following passage (although they were made often enough) for obvious reasons.

thing. . . . Of course we have had our troubles in other societies, but I think they have got more respect for what has got to happen, even if you get a man who is not a good co-operative man . . .[6]

In other words it was only in Kandara that some committee members were from the outset prepared for direct conflict with the Co-operative Department and the Union. During 1967 the Kandara activists recruited much support from other societies, at the same time that the Kandara KANU leaders gathered district-wide support in their fight against planting restrictions. But while they could gain recruits for their attacks on the Union, actual defiance of the legal provisions was largely confined to Kandara, which both Kebatta and the Co-operative Officer had identified as the 'problem area' at an early stage. This defiance, during early 1967, took the form of a simple refusal to obey the Co-operative Officer's demand that they order all supplies through the Union.

But for the Kandara committees to continue independent purchasing involved breach of another rule: that which required all financial instruments to be countersigned by the Co-operative Officer and by Kebatta as Union secretary-manager. Aside from the breach of law involved, and the fact that the committee members were laying themselves open to surcharge, there was the added difficulty that both banks in Fort Hall, Barclays D.C.O. and National & Grindlays, had agreed in February to refuse payment on any cheques from primary societies which were not countersigned.[7] The societies concerned were largely successful in circumventing this difficulty, however, by not banking cash payments made to them for fertilizer, seedlings, etc. (thereby violating yet another rule), and making payment to their wholesalers in cash.

It has been noted earlier that as far as day-to-day control of primary society affairs was concerned, the role of government officers was marginal, since the Union had been willy-nilly recruited to perform the functions of reform and regulation. The Murang'a Union, however, possessed features which ensured that the manner in which changes were made, and the reactions that they provoked, differed substantially from government intentions. Members of the management committee of the Union had to fill two uncomfortably contradictory roles—as policy makers on various issues critical to co-operative development in the district, and as chairmen of primary societies whose committees were often adversely affected by Union supervision of their affairs, and by the policies decided on in the Union. It was difficult for Union

[6] June 23rd, 1967.
[7] Barclay's Bank manager, Fort Hall, April 1967.

management committee members to refuse to take decisions enforcing the Co-operative Society Rules and government policy on such matters as free tendering for supplies, particularly when government officers— the Co-operative Officer, often the Coffee Officer and occasionally the DC himself—attended their meetings, and when decisions had to be recorded and subsequently approved by the Commissioner for Co-operative Development. Clearly, however, the chairmen could not hope to (and in many cases probably did not wish to) persuade their primary society committees to accept these decisions, particularly on such sensitive matters as the centralization of coffee seedlings and the ordering of supplies.

Thus while Kebatta could rely on his management committee to accord him formal powers to carry out what was required of the Union government and by the Union's own internal needs, he was acutely conscious even in early 1967 that he could not rely on them for support in a confrontation with primary societies. More than that, Kebatta felt that the management committee members were deliberately restricting their role on these controversial issues to the bare minimum required of them, and were not even prepared to act as channels of communication between Union and primaries in the implementation of Union policy.

> Our members (of the management committee) are never really firm in their decisions. They will pass things here in the boardroom because there is no alternative to what must be done—they know that we have to do these things we don't want—but then they are swayed by their members, and some of them there in Kandara will even be working against them (the decisions) as soon as they leave here. You can see that we even have to keep on writing all these letters to them as chairmen of their societies, even if we see them here every week or two. If we don't do this we cannot be sure that they will feel all right to say these things to their committee members and the ordinary growers—even if the things are not very unpopular, just ordinary administrative matters of the Union . . .
> So really this Union must be run by myself with just a few staff . . . of course the committee is still the head, and I don't ever think these matters are passed at the meetings and then the delegates are even a bit surprised in their own areas when we come to act on them![8]

It might have seemed, then, that Kebatta was in a strong position to be the dominant figure in the Union, and by implication in Murang'a

---

[8] Kebatta, March 1967.

co-operative affairs. The formalistic resolutions of the Union management committee gave to his actions the sanction he required, while individually and collectively members shrank from exercising control within the Union over their implementation. But the disadvantage, from the secretary-manager's point of view, sprang from that same fact, that the committee's decisions on critical issues of co-operative reform and coffee control were made, so to speak, for appearance's sake: while he might have had sanction for his actions, Kebata lacked allies among Murang'a's most powerful co-operative leaders. During 1967, as the campaigns against the Union and the government gathered force, he did indeed seek allies among the management committee members, with some success; nevertheless, his most substantial support lay outside the Union itself, in Murang'a government departments, among the Fort Hall town business community, and in such Nairobi bodies as the Coffee Board of Kenya and the Kenya Planters' Co-operative Union.[9]

The Coffee Factories Dispute

The threat to primary society growers and committee members posed by new government controls over coffee planting and co-operative

[9] Kebatta was born in the town, the son of an African stallholder, and is in his early fifties. He had spent seven years from 1940 in the Post Office in Dar es Salaam, followed by two years in Nairobi as a legal clerk in a firm of solicitors. In 1949 he was appointed Fort Hall African Courts Registrar, and in 1953 Clerk to the African District Council. A marginal involvement in nationalist politics led to him being detained from 1954 to 1956, when he was released with full 'security clearance', and from 1957 to 1960 he worked as a farm planning assistant in the Fort Hall Department of Agriculture. Although this was a minor post for a man of his experience, it had offered him the opportunity of extending contacts with the African farming community, so that he was employed by Mugoiri Co-operative Society early in 1960. While holding this post, he played a major role in the formation of the Union, particularly in drawing up applications to the Commissioner for Co-operative Development, and in drafting other legal documents. He was appointed secretary-manager when the Union was registered late in 1960, and in the following year spent four months in Israel on a co-operative training course. In the first County Council elections in 1963, Kebatta was elected for Fort Hall township, although he did not stand again in 1966. In 1964 he went on another training course, this time to South Korea.

Kebatta had possessed a number of desirable qualifications for the post of secretary-manager; administrative ability, legal training, and extensive contacts both among coffee growers and among the Government extension staff. In political terms he must also have seemed a wise choice: he had never been closely associated with the colonial regime, or at least with the most contentious aspects of colonial administration. He had been detained for nationalist sympathies, but was not a 'die-hard' who might have created difficulties both with the colonial authorities and with the loyalists who constituted a powerful section of the Murang'a's co-operative movement, particularly in Kandara.

administration immediately jeopardized both the Union's effectiveness and Kebatta's own position: the latter control placed the Union and its secretary-manager at the centre of conflict by devolving heavy responsibilities on them, and the coffee control issue was swiftly taken up by politicians within and outside the co-operative movement as ammunition against the Union. During 1967, the Union's opponents sought to manipulate Union finances to maintain their illegal sources of wealth, and they 'politicized' their difference with the Union by linking it with the control of coffee planting. Besides trying to evade the Rules about supply ordering and counter-signature of cheques, some co-operative committees also appear to have extended their activities into the field of coffee factory construction. Coffee factories in African areas were financed by loans from the new Coffee Authority, whose primary purpose was to ensure the rapid development of existing factories and drying tables belonging to primary societies, and the construction where appropriate of new ones, to meet the large increase in crop anticipated from 1967 onward.[10] By March 1967 the Authority and its predecessors in this field had already approved £222,675 in loans to Murang'a co-operatives for coffee factory construction and extension. Thirty-eight factories were already operational in the district, with 33 under construction, and a further 10 proposed.[11] Of the sum approved, approximately £90,000 had not yet been disbursed.[12]

Co-operative societies had an obvious interest in increasing the processing facilities in the district: not only would the increased capacity improve cherry quality and thereby increase returns, but growers (usually the women) would not have to carry the heavy sacks of cherry for long distances to central processing and drying centres. For the individual committee member, there were the less tangible advantages of prestige and popularity in securing the building of a factory to the benefit of his neighbours. But for those committee members who had indulged in the personal discount system or in similar activities at the expense of their growers, the construction of processing facilities, necessitating buying machinery and building materials, hiring labour and awarding contracts, appeared to offer further prospects of personal enrichment, and there is little doubt that some primary society committees took advantage of it where they could.

But the expanded factory programme of the Coffee Authority

[10] Coffee Board of Kenya *Annual Report* for 1966.
[11] *Kenya Coffee,* April 1967. The large expansion of processing facilities which would more than double the number of factories in Murang'a was a direct result of the establishment of the Coffee Authority.
[12] District Agricultural Officer, Murang'a, April 1967.

brought with it stricter controls over the spending of loan money, controls which parallelled those established by the Co-operative Societies Rules. In this case, payments in connection with coffee factory construction had to be approved by the District Agricultural Officer or his appointed substitute—in Murang'a, the Cash Crops Officer was charged with this responsibility.

During the last quarter of 1966, there was a substantial number of cases of societies paying very high prices for construction materials and coffee machinery, but the Department of Agriculture was not yet in a position to exercise effective control over payments, since societies' general funds were not yet under the control of the Co-operative Officer and the Union.[13] But by the time of the Union meeting of January 14th, 1967, the Department was able to issue a strong warning to the primary societies—a warning which, even in the truncated form of the minutes of the meeting, barely avoided acknowledging that misappropriation was taking place.

> Cash Crops Officer Mr Williams informed the meeting that Murang'a co-operatives had applied for all the amount allocated to the district, and warned that unless societies spent this loan money properly, factories already started may remain uncompleted for lack of money.
>
> He pointed out that a number of Societies had appeared to be spending the money in some unnecessary parts of buildings and also paying costly for things which could be paid for with reasonable and normal price.
>
> He reminded the meeting that he would not be approving payments for things that showed higher prices than they should.[14]

At the same meeting, however, members of the management committee secured for their societies some funds which were not so controlled: they resolved that £3,125 should be paid, *pro rata* to Union levy contributions, to primary societies out of the Union's balance of cash at the close of the previous financial year. The purpose of this payment was quite explicitly to circumvent the tighter controls—'owing to difficulties societies were experiencing for handy cash for immediate purchase of coffee factories materials.'[15] There was nothing improper in the committee deciding to redistribute to member societies a part of its surplus, nor in the societies using the cash for coffee factory construction. In the case of most of the societies, the purpose of the cash distribution would indeed be to ease the inevitable delays involved

---

[13] DAO Murang'a, April 1967.
[14] Minute 341/67 (4).
[15] Minute 345/67.

in Government officers checking and approving orders before materials could be delivered. It seems clear that only a minority—albeit a politically important one—had personal interests in unsupervised purchases.

The Union payment was in any case so small by the time it was broken down for payment to individual societies as to make the opportunity for profit negligible. What it did offer, however, was a convenient opportunity for subsequent attacks on the Union: at growers' meetings in Kandara a few months later, this payment was said to be 'all that could be got out of Kebatta' of the coffee loan money which rightfully belonged to the primary societies.

This sort of allegation was of a piece with the other attacks on the Union and on Kebatta by politicians and co-operative leaders for their real or imagined associations with government actions, and it is important in that context. But it also reflected the real resentment of committees against what they felt to be the imposition on their societies of unfair arrangements for financing coffee factory construction. The government's aims of expanding factory facilities while ensuring careful control of expenditure and the prompt repayment of loans were implemented by making the loans through the unpopular Coffee Authority, controlling their disbursement through the local officials of the Department of Agriculture, and having repayment instalments deducted by the Coffee Marketing Board from growers' proceeds. The Union could thus be plausibly associated with these arrangements, since it was the Union which received the Marketing Board payouts net of loan instalments. In addition, the expenditure control procedure meant that in many cases primary societies were paying instalments on loans which had not yet been disbursed: an Agriculture Department official cited the case of a society which had spent nothing of a £3,000 loan, but which had already 'repaid' £375. The anger which these arrangements provoked is reflected in the resolutions passed at each of the Union meetings referred to in the previous chapter—resolutions which not only demanded that the practice of automatic deduction of loan instalments by the Marketing Board should stop, but which stipulated that the amounts involved should be repaid with interest to those societies which had not been able to draw on their loan allocations because of delays in the checking procedure.

The loans issue was also political, however, in the sense that it involved arguments about the control of co-operative resources and the legitimate scope of intervention by the Union and by the government. The Kandara group, certainly, viewed it as integral to their campaign.

> Our farmers here have suffered quite a lot because of all this interference with our affairs.... We were always speaking out

that there was too much interference, and now the growers are finding that they get very low payments from the Union, because the money is being held back for these loans which the societies never received. . . . They all must say yes before anything can be done—Kebatta wants to see all the invoices, and then the Department of Agriculture, and everybody, and the factories cannot be put up. But all the time our money is going out. But we are the people who were elected, and up to now we can do nothing to do our jobs properly.[16]

Kariuki's phrasing is revealing: some responsibility for the delays and deductions was being assigned to the Union by the dissidents in the growers' meetings and KANU rallies, although they well knew that it bore none. As in the case of other allegations made against it, however, the Union could be cast in this role, firstly because rank and file growers had no clear idea of the quite complex administrative relationships between the various bodies concerned with the co-operatives, and secondly, because committee members themselves had been made increasingly conscious of the Union's new role of executor of government policy. With the Union being placed in a position of general responsibility for primary society affairs, its opponents were unlikely to draw fine distinctions in their propaganda against it.

Struggle within the Union

By the time Kandara co-operative leaders began their campaign against planting restrictions, the Co-operative Officer's circular of January 10th had already produced strong reactions from the primary societies. A deputation of three Kandara societies visited the Union chairman, Karugu, to protest at the Union's endorsement of the Rules (despite the fact that their chairmen, who were among the protesters, had voted to adopt the Rules in the Union management committee); they were particularly incensed at Kebatta 'giving them orders'.[17] Other societies, too, not all of them in Kandara, had complained that the Union was acting 'like part of the government', and was no longer defending growers' interests as it had in the past. This sentiment was critical to the success of the Kandara group's campaigns for local co-operative autonomy and against the planting restrictions. It seems, however, that in the initial stages of the group's efforts to recruit allies among the other co-operative leaders the anti-Union content of their arguments was relatively small.

They were saying that we must all be united to make our voice

[16] Jasmel Kariuki, May 20th, 1967.
[17] Karugu, April 21st, 1967.

clear to the Government that these restrictions must stop. But also it afterwards became a thing of being against the Union in everything we did. They said that we were taking members' money away, and that now we wanted to take away their seedlings, and we were just working against the local people as we were told by the Coffee Board.[18]

There was no clearly discernible reason for this change in emphasis; it is conceivable that the involvement of the Kandara KANU leadership in the anti-restriction meetings and rallies entailed some toning-down of direct attacks on the government; the interests of the politicians and of Kandara primary society committees thus coincided in placing increased emphasis on the alleged responsibility of the Union for growers' grievances—an evocative theme even with those primary society committees which did not have a direct political or pecuniary interest in attacking the Union.

Throughout the period we are discussing, it was the Kandara KANU leadership, and not the party leadership in the district in general, which was most actively involved in the co-operative disputes: although the non-Kandara MPs gave the anti-restriction campaign their tacit blessing, and although county councillors and KANU officials from other parts of the district gave their support to the coffee growers, they appeared to do so as a response to pressure from growers in their own areas—and to protect themselves from subversion by the Mwaura group.

The critical point in the conflict within the movement was the KANU-inspired growers' meeting of May 6th—the meeting which also produced, as we have seen, the most strident and most widely-based protests against planting restrictions. The Union was subjected to bitter attacks from committeemen and from KANU officials, and Kebatta was personally singled out for 'working against the growers'. Karugu, the Union chairman, and Kebatta both addressed the meeting, but apparently made little impression.

> Some of these Kandara people started saying that I was trying to centralize supply ordering and so forth in the Union because I was being paid by Dalgety's to give them orders, and was taking bribes, because the Union tenders from them. But you know yourself that a big firm like that does not have to worry about bribing people, and even then every penny must be shown, how it has been spent. It is these Asian family shops in Thika, they are the ones who can give bribes, and the people who are accusing me are themselves the fools of these Asians. And the worst thing was that some of the people who were there shouting against me for corruption were members of the Union committee, and they were

[18] Kebatta, June 23rd, 1967.

even present here in the offices when all those tenders were opened! Anyhow I told them all these things, but no-one wanted to listen to us, and afterwards these politicians just got up and started to whip up feelings against the Union again.[19]

The District Commissioner's decision after May 6th that there should be a meeting between Union, primary societies and KANU leaders may well have been prompted from Nairobi: Murang'a had already emerged as the focal point of protest against planting restrictions, and the growers were being led by politicians whose allegiance to Kiano, the Murang'a politician closest to the President, was dubious. From the DC's own viewpoint, in any case, there were clearly good reasons for wanting to curtail the conflict. Although the Union was not the pliable instrument of government which the Kandara people painted it as, it was more amenable to argument and persuasion by the Co-operative and Agriculture Departments, and had close working relationships with them. Apart from the fact that it possessed better resources—of money, equipment and skills—than the primary societies, it was felt that Union control of the kind provided for in the Co-operative Societies Rules would help to ensure a balance between local interests and national development policy. Administrators pointed to the 'selfishness' of primary society leaders, and to the difficulties of supervision and liaison if control of co-operative resources was diffused in a large number of small organizations scattered throughout the district. Moreover, the instrusion of KANU activists into co-operative conflicts was unwelcome to the Administration: there was the feeling that KANU representatives were 'meddling', that they were treading on the toes of the civil service and 'harming the development of the district'[20], which often, in administrative minds, came to the same thing.

While Koinange (the DC) was concerned to contain anti-Union feeling, however, he was also aware of the political sensitivity of the co-operative reform issue, and of the considerable influence of dissidents such as Ndung'u Kagori. His speech to the 'peace conference' on May 20th was thus conciliatory in tone, although it made the Administration's essential points about observance of the law.[21] Thus, for example, he did not openly defend Kebatta, but advised society delegates 'not to be swayed into cheap allegations against their staff'; he did not accuse primary society chairmen of reneging on their decisions

---

[19] Kebatta, June 23rd, 1967.
[20] This is a summary of conversation with a number of administrative and technical officers during May 1967.
[21] The account of the DC's speech is drawn from the very full minutes of this meeting, afterwards checked with Koinange for accuracy. Subsequent references to speeeches at the meeting also refer to reports in the minutes, similarly checked.

in the Union management committee, but noted that 'misunderstandings sometimes arose because society members were not fully informed about what had been decided at Union meetings, and so were sometimes confused as to who really decided on various policies'; and so forth.

The Union Chairman, Samuel Karugu, gave a comprehensive defence of the Union's position, commenting on each of the allegations against the Union made at the earlier growers' conference. Karugu's main concern, however, was to reach an accommodation with the Party which would protect the Union, Kebatta and himself from further political attack, and at the same time further the cause against planting restrictions. He attempted to define the different fields of concern of the co-operatives and KANU—'KANU was a political party now running Government of the country, while co-operatives were organizations for economic developments in the country and the district'—but conceded that KANU, as the representative of the people, had the right to be consulted and to work with the Union 'in all matters of general problems of public interest in the district'.[21]

Although the KANU leadership and the Kandara co-operative activists at the meeting were influential in getting critical resolutions passed in spite of the District Administration's intervention, the tone of the meeting was certainly far more moderate and conciliatory than the earlier KANU-convened one had been. The KANU speakers—Wanjagi, Mwaura, Thabuni and Kamau Njoroge—now all asserted that they had no quarrel with the Union 'as such'; what they were concerned about were complaints from growers about delayed payment of coffee proceeds, about infill restrictions and uprooting, and about high Union prices for supplies.

The KANU leadership obviously shared the Union's concern that there should be at least the semblance of a united front between party and growers' organization in opposing planting restrictions, particularly since the Kandara party notables at any rate had a directly personal interest in defeating the restrictions. In local political terms, their counciliatory attitude stemmed from the fact that their campaign had largely succeeded. The Kandara group had swung the majority of the primary societies behind its campaign, and had likewise compelled the KANU organization outside the division to support it—a significant victory, given the subordinate position of the 'Mwaura faction' at this time, and given that KANU in the other divisions was not identified with the wealthier farmers to the extent that it was in Kandara. Perhaps most importantly of all, the Union, by convening the May 20th meeting, acknowledged that the co-operatives were not solely the business of the co-operators—that political conflicts affected co-operative administration, and that therefore politicians and their interests were matters of importance. Both Mwaura and Kamau Njoroge had made this point at the meeting (although Karugu had tried to rebut it), and Njoroge had proposed that KANU leaders should be invited to participate in Union meetings 'for exchanging views that concerned interests of the public in the district'. Although the proposal was not put as a formal resolution, it was understood that there would be periodic joint meetings in the future.

Policy Changes and Local Power

The outcome of the growers' campaign which had culminated in this meeting has already been related, insofar as planting restrictions are concerned. The government's reversal of policy on this issue has been pointed to as the clearest example of the influence which Murang'a politicians were able to exert on central government development policy. Their influence in modifying government action on the other issues described in this chapter and in the preceding one was more diffuse: certain government actions might plausibly be said to have been influenced by the Murang'a campaign, but in no case was government's response so unequivocal or immediate as it had been in prohibiting the uprooting of African coffee.

When Gichuru announced that there would be no more uprooting, he also gave an undertaking that the government would abolish or suspend the coffee export tax of £20 a ton when the price fell below £320 per ton—a concession which, while the tax had not been much talked of among growers' complaints, did represent a potential easing of growers' financial burden, and would help to reassure them about their incomes in the event of a drop in world prices.[22] Some months later, it was announced that the Coffee Marketing Board and the Coffee Board of Kenya were to be disbanded, and a single new board set up in their place—although the Coffee Authority, the object of African criticism, remained in being.[23] Thus while the complaints about the existence and operation of the Authority—not only from Murang'a but from other coffee districts as well—did not succeed, some concession was made to the feeling among growers that they supported an expensive and oppressive bureaucratic structure.

In terms of local politics, however, and in terms of the effects of these conflicts on the activities of government officers in the district

---

[22] I have not seen any evidence that the tax was a very contentious issue, either in Murang'a or elsewhere. The proferred abolition was most probably intended as evidence of the government's mollifying attitude towards the disaffected growers.

[23] Coffee Board of Kenya announcement, published in *Kenya Coffee*, November 1967.

the issues of co-operative reform and coffee control effected marked changes. In the first place, the political activity centring on these issues in Murang'a had established the commanding position of Kandara leaders within the district co-operative movement—a predominance which was further confirmed in their subsequent ability to call Kebatta to account. The Kandara co-operative leaders had been able to mobilize the political resources of the division's KANU organization in support of their campaigns and in support of their personal economic interests. By politicizing the issues in this way, they had ensured the defeat of planting control, and had been able to maintain at least some of the economic and political advantages to themselves which the co-operative reforms had been designed to abolish.

The government officers charged with responsibility for coffee control had been eager to disengage themselves from direct surveillance of the growers, partly because of a certain lack of confidence in their own cause, in that Agriculture officials were in some doubt about the accuracy of their tree census figures. More important however, was their clear realization that the control of illegal planting was not simply a matter of administrative implementation, but had important political implications: officers were concerned that the coffee issue would impinge on other departmental programmes, and that they would provoke hostility, exacerbated by political agitation, towards all their activities in the district. Significantly, agricultural officers' uncertainty over the issue was often expressed by reference to the District Commissioner having 'failed to give a lead': in other words, the DC's reticence was (rightly) interpreted as evidence of the political sensitivity of the issue. If the President's personal representative in the district did not unequivocally demand growers' compliance with planting regulations, it meant that the activities of Murang'a notables were having effect at State House.

The Co-operative Officer was on rather firmer ground in implementing the Rules, since here there was no attempt to invoke *Mzee's* authority against the reforms. Moreover, the DC had in this case publicly demanded obedience to government policy and the law. Nevertheless, as the foregoing narrative has shown, the Co-operative staff were offending the same influential figures who had induced such circumspection in the Agriculture officials; moreover, in the minds of ordinary growers at least, the two issues were inextricably intertwined. And in this case again, officers felt that precipitate action might jeopardize their efforts in other fields.

> We have been trying for some time to get the Union to form a credit society, because then the farmers will be able to get some small sums for improving their *shambas* and caring for their trees

> properly, and so on. Now last year they registered one and it has been working quite well. But all these fellows are well represented, and they could easily make quite a lot of trouble.... You see, before you can get a loan (from the credit society) you must be recommended by the management of that primary society you belong to, and then it can only be used for improving a *shamba,* and so on. But it's very easy to start messing around with this money, although so far we haven't had any trouble, and are watching it very closely.[24]

Because of these potential problems, and because of the statutory provisions placing the burden of co-operative administration on the Union rather than on government officers, Co-operative Department officials in Murang'a were emphatic that their role was one of advising societies on management, consulting with the Union on Murang'a co-operative affairs, and exercising supervision only in a broad sense: the District Co-operative Officer contended that day-to-day problems, 'including all these troubles between the Union and the members over supplies and so forth',[25] should be dealt with by Kebatta and his staff. The Co-operative Department was prepared to issue circulars and make public pronouncements on appropriate occasions calling for the obedience of primary societies, but it did not wish to intervene when disputes arose. Primary society leaders in fact had little to say on the role of the Co-operative Department in implementing the reforms— Kebatta was the one who was said to be 'obstructive' about counter-signing orders, demanding monthly trial balances and minutes of meetings, and so forth. Several Union management committee members asserted that the Co-operative Officer would only stop payment on primary society cheques on Kebatta's recommendation but the Co-operative Officer asserted that he had refused counter-signature on eleven orders, valued at over £700, during the first three months of 1967, depite Kebatta's recommendation that they be passed.[26] In spite of this, the differing interpretations of the Rules and of government policy provoked disagreement between the Co-operative Department and Kebatta—especially as the latter came to see himself more isolated and prone to attack from the Kandara primary societies.

> It's all right to say the Union must run the affairs of the co-operatives, and anyway that is what we are doing but these supervisory jobs put a big strain on our staff. We are just going around checking, so that even when we employ someone for training people in co-operative principles and so forth you will

[24] District Co-operative Officer, April 1967.
[25] Ibid.
[26] Ibid.

find that he spends most of his time working on supervision, so that there is nearly no training being done at present. But anyway we are just staff, and when these fights come up about the Rules and so on, you can't say that our staff must be involved to that extent. These are the Government's Rules, and the Co-operative Officer must be here to see that they go through.[27]

Despite the reluctance of the Co-operative Department to become involved in the ongoing disputes between the Union and the primary societies, however, there can be little doubt that the Department's support for Kebatta helped to preserve him in office in the critical period of May 1967 and immediately thereafter. The Co-operative Officer felt that, apart from Kebatta's ability as an administrator, the government had specifically stated that it would protect society employees from dismissal for refusing to exercise favouritism towards committee members[28]: and the same applied to an employee who refused to depart from the Co-operative Society Rules.[29] Even more important, the DC's public support for this view at the May 20th meeting gave to the Co-operative Department the political authority to warn committee members privately that the Commissioner for Co-operative Development would refuse to sanction Kebatta's dismissal.[30]

It is an open question whether the Kandara co-operative leaders would otherwise have secured it. What they did do, however, was to emphasize his status as being subordinate to the Union management committee, to reassert the elective nature of the Union's management and, by implication, to reassert that power and authority flowed upward from the primary societies, and not downward from the Union. With the planting restriction battle safely won, the management committee met on June 10th to consider allegations made against Kebatta. Kandara members of the committee charged that

> 1. Union General Secretary-Manager was controlling the Committee when it was committee which should have been controlling him.
>
> 2. General Secretary-Manager had much of his time with (Coffee) Board (of Kenya) meetings.
>
> 3. General Secretary-Manager had connections with Messrs.

---

[27] Kebata, May 12th, 1967.
[28] See Development Plan, p. 200.
[29] Co-operative Officer, July 1967.
[30] The committee member who told me this said there had been similar warnings 'from even higher up'.

Dalgety (E.A.) Ltd. and was therefore making societies buy from this company than from other suppliers.

4. Purchases were being made without knowledge of management committee.[31]

These allegations were in effect a summary of those made against Kebatta in the political campaigns of previous months. It did not matter that Kebatta could and did rebut them in detail; they were more important for what they signified than for what they alleged. Thus while Kebatta could truthfully argue that he did not 'control the committee' because the only action he took was in accordance with committee resolutions and directives, he knew as well as his accusers did that many of these resolutions were passed merely to comply with the law or in deference to government pressure: especially where measures of centralizing control were involved, primary society leaders had had no intention of allowing the control of their resources and their afffairs to pass to the Union. Kebatta had taken management committee decision at face value in order to implement reform; he was now being called to account.

Similarly, the assertion that he spent too much time attending Coffee Board meetings was an oblique repetition of earlier criticisms that Kebatta was too closely associated with the 'coffee bureaucracy', that he had ceased to represent the Union's interest and had been absorbed into an apparatus which the growers felt to be oppressive. The allegation that Kebatta had improper connections with Dalgety's has been referred to earlier: its repetition at this meeting could only have been intended to emphasize the fact that Kebatta was being disciplined for his actions in attempting to stop primary societies ordering their own supplies. As Kebatta pointed out at the meeting, the Union's trading relationship with Dalgety's had been established when he was in South Korea, and the most recent supply contract has been awarded to Dalgety's by a sub-committee of the Union management committee set up to supervise tender procedures.

Kebatta had rebutted all the charges in considerable detail, apparently without provoking further criticisms from the meeting. Yet he was refused a vote of confidence when he asked for one: the committee stated that it would 'see how things went'.[32]

The co-operative reform issue thus had not been resolved. Kebatta was still in post, despite the hostility of the most influential co-operative leaders, and could not be dismissed—in that respect,

[31] Meeting of the management committee of MFCU Ltd. June 10th, 1967. Min. 367/67.
[32] Private communication. This information does not appear in the minutes of the meeting which were drafted, as usual, by Kebatta.

government reform measures had effected an important change. There was no evidence that he would no longer attempt to enforce the Co-operative Society Rules—but equally co-operative leaders had ensured that any reforming efforts by Kebatta would be bitterly contested by the primary societies, while Kebatta could not hope, at that stage at least, for a great deal of support from the Co-operative Department.

The most influential co-operative leaders had been able to mobilize powerful political resources to defeat planting restrictions, thereby protecting their own interests and enhancing their status among their members; at the same time, that issue had assisted their efforts to maintain control of co-operative resources. The opportunities for personal enrichment from primary society committee membership had been substantially reduced (although not entirely eradicated), but the success of the Kandara group offered ample evidence of the continuing importance of primary societies in political terms: the local societies offered an organized and relatively wealthy constituency of political support, and leadership roles in them conferred social status and— particularly in Kandara—the possibility of political advancement. This political aspect will again be considered in the following chapter.

Chapter VII

POWER, DEVELOPMENT AND POLITICAL CHANGE

The account of Kenyan and Murang'a politics in the preceding chapters has emphasized three related themes: the divided character of the Kenyan political movement as it developed in response to colonial conquest, the emergence of social class as a principle of political recruitment, and the growing importance, locally as well as nationally, of ideology as a distinguishing criterion in political conflict. An attempt can now be made to assess the impact of these factors on the 'development' activities of government discussed above, and to relate the Murang'a experience to the general pattern of Kenyan economic and political change.

In doing so, however, it is important to have as precise an idea as possible of the substantive basis on which Murang'a politicians based their class-oriented political appeals: and here, as in most underdeveloped countries, data on stratification and class formation are hard to come by and often dated or otherwise unreliable. Reference to Chapter 1 will indicate the heavy reliance on Sorrenson's work for information about social change during the Emergency. The evidence which Sorrenson adduces may be briefly summarized as follows: the land consolidation programme initiated during the Emergency was designed to create a class of large Kikuyu landowners employing substantial numbers of agricultural labourers and buttressed, in a socio-political sense, by a much larger class of peasants owning their land and depending on their own labour and that of their families to work it. The *ahoi*, the 'terrorists' and those whose land claims were marginal or dubious would be transformed into labourers for the rural bourgeoisie.

To carry our knowledge forward in time, there is one further major source of evidence about social structure which can be drawn on: the Economic Survey of Central Province 1963-64.[1] This was a survey, over

---

[1] Statistics Division, Ministry of Economic Planning and Development, Nairobi 1968.

a period of a year, of the economy of some 900 sample rural households in the province. It is subject, of course, to sampling error—particularly where the total is broken down into district and other kinds of categories. It is also dated, a particularly important point when one remembers that the major expansion in African agricultural production (especially in Murang'a) took place after 1964. Nevertheless, it is appropriate to discuss the Survey's findings at some length, since its figures about wealth, income and land distribution are of particular relevance to the issues of class and ideology stressed in this book.

For present purposes, the most important body of evidence in the Survey is that relating to the distribution of land. This effectively disposes of whatever is left of the notion of a peasant community with relatively equal distribution of land and wealth: although there is little evidence of the evolution of a large-capitalist or a *rentier* class, there is every indication of wide disparities in holding and wealth, if the Survey data are generally replicated in Central Province.

Furthermore, economic cleavages are more marked and disparities wider in Murang'a than in any other district in the Province. The largest land operators,[2] those operating 20 acres or more, constituted only 1.6% of all sample households; but this upper section of the rural population operated no less than 8.1% of the total land area operated by all households. In Murang'a the large land-operators (more than 20 acres) are more numerous—3.8%, and this group operated almost one-quarter of all land under use in Murang'a. At the other end of the scale, the smallest land operators—less than two acres—constituted 31.8% of all households in the Province; yet they operated only 13.1% of all land under use. In Murang'a, these very small operators accounted for a slightly lower proportion of all households, (26.4%), but a *much* lower proportion of total acreage—a mere 4.7%.[3]

The biggest category of peasant households—some 50%—operated between 2 and 6 acres: in the Province as a whole this half of the peasantry operated a commensurate proportion of the total land area—again, just under half. In the case of Murang'a, however, the 48.8% of peasant households operating between 2 and 6 acres operated only 34% of the land.

In short, the differences between Murang'a and the rest of Central Province go some way towards explaining why social conflict should

---

[2] 'Land operated' was defined as '... the area of all land, owned or otherwise, which was wholly or partly used for cultivation or for other purposes by the household'. *Survey,* p. 19.

[3] Calculated from *Survey,* op. cit., tables at p. 21, of (a) Distribution of households operating land, by size of holding, and (b) Distribution of total acreage operated, by size of holding.

occur in that district rather than elsewhere. Large land operators were more numerous in the district, and controlled much more of the land available. The small and middle peasantry in Murang'a, while constituting a proportion of the population similar to their counterparts in other districts, controlled a much smaller proportion of the land: hence, average individual landholdings among these groups in Murang'a were much smaller, within each category (less than 2 acres; 2-6 acres), than elsewhere.

The comparative distribution of land between large and small operators can be succinctly expressed. Looking at the distribution of the total land acreage under use between these groups. the following (rounded) figures emerge. Holdings of less than 6 acres: Kiambu 81%, Embu 57%, Nyeri 70%, Meru 61%, *Murang'a 38%.* Holdings of ten acres and above: Kiambu 8%, Embu 21%, Nyeri 19%, Meru 20%, *Murang'a 39%.*

This is persuasive, albeit incomplete, evidence of the social basis for political conflict in Murang'a, at least where the crucial resource of land was concerned. And one might reasonably assume that. if these orders of magnitude have changed in the ensuing years, they have changed in the direction of less equality in land ownership rather than more, with the growth of an urban salaried elite which nevertheless retains strong rural links, and which can and does siphon considerable urban resources into rural land purchase.

Land ownership or land operation was not the only source of wealth in Murang'a, however; and indeed the Survey suggests not only that productivity per acre falls off markedly with increases in farm size, but that, for the wealthiest households, manufacturing, trade and transport and wage employment, formed a much larger proportion of total income than agricultural receipts.[4] Nevertheless, large landholdings were clearly a concomitant of wealth.[5] The figures indicate, if anything, that those households which dominated the agricultural sector because of the size of their holdings also tended to control most rural commerce, particularly retailing and transport, and to be most advantageously placed (mainly through education, no doubt) to secure wage employment.

The picture which emerges, therefore, is of an upper stratum in Murang'a which exercised much greater leverage over critical rural resources than did the great bulk of the peasantry. They do not appear to be so much a bourgeoisie as a peasant elite or leadership, taking advantage of a number of different income-producing activities, of

---

[4] *Survey,* p. 39. Note, though, that the agricultural expansion of the 1960's would almost certainly be an increase in the productivity of larger holdings relative to smaller ones.

[5] Ibid.

which those of a specifically *capitalist* nature were only a part. That this group was attempting to transform itself into a bourgeoisie is clear, not only from the actions of individuals in Murang'a, but from the fact that the utilization of hired labour in agriculture accounted for fully 15% of the total labour input on farms of 8 acres and above,[6] and that over half of the total cash receipts of the richest group came from activities with a high hired labour content—manufacturing, trade and transport.[7]

But aside from the 'observer's' model of the Murang'a social order alluded to in the foregoing paragraphs, there is the critical issue of class consciousness—of people's perception of themselves in relation to their social environment, and in particular of their perception of the criteria by which resources are (or ought to be) allocated to individuals and groups. It is plain, from the account of local political conflict in chapter 3, that Murang'a politicians clearly perceived that class interests were at issue in their rivalries.

The Structure of Conflict

Initially, Kaggia's articulation of the ex-detainees' grievances camouflaged the issue in a way which alluded to the divisions which had long existed in the Kikuyu political movement, and which had been complicated and exacerbated by the Emergency. At first it was only his faction within KANU which tried to champion the cause of particular social groups, while his opponents still relied on the themes of national unity and Kikuyu reunification. In the course of political conflict in the district after independence, however, Kiano and his supporters were compelled to identify their potential followers more exactly, and to try to ensure that they, rather than Kaggia, secured the allegiances of the majority of small landowners.[8]

It would be wrong, however, to infer from this line of argument that social class 'simplified' political allegiance in the factional competition in Murang'a. While it is true that Kaggia's supporters, once he came under strong pressure from factional opponents after 1964, could be fairly accurately defined as poor, landless or owning very little land, and predominantly ex-detainee, it has earlier been stressed that the social composition of the leadership of the opposing faction, and of the groups from which it drew support, were more diverse. Thus, in the 1961 to 1964 period, Kaggia was the leader of what was, in Bruce Graham's terms,[9] a faction with a direct structure—that is, its

[6] Ibid., p. 15.
[7] Ibid., p. 41.
[8] See especially pp. 35-38 above.
[9] B. D. Graham in *Local-Level Politics,* op. cit., p. 324.

secondary leaders were his lieutenants, and his followers owed direct allegiance to Kaggia himself. In this period, Kaggia could and did recruit followers 'on simple and specialized terms',[10] and on diverse principles[11]: he could command allegiance not only because of his support for the cause of the landless and ex-detainees, but because he offered aspirant politicians (his faction's 'core') the possibility of office within the KANU organization, because he could offer employment (for example, his house in Kandara was built by local labour, using locally-produced material where possible), or help with land problems through his activism in challenging land consolidation errors and injustices. Kaggia was prepared, however, to expend political resources by refusing to compromise on the issues of land and (in Parliament) nationalization and socialism, and in this preparedness was the more vulnerable to the activities of his enemies in Kandara and to the sharpening ideological cleaveages in Nairobi, which also had their effect on local politics.

The structure of the Kiano faction, by contrast, was indirect—that is, it was an alliance of more than one faction, with at least one secondary leader (Mwaura) possessing the capacity to break away and maintain an independent existence, even though the political costs of doing so would have been high. The immediate assumption could be that Mwaura's independence, such as it was, stemmed from his control of political resources in a specific geographical area (Kandara), rather than of a particular category of people: it is indicated below that this explanation is oversimplified.

In a structural sense, therefore, the Kiano faction (or alliance) embodied within itself the possibility of fission and a new system of factional conflict—a possibility which was realized, to a limited extent, in the attempt to subvert Kiano's leadership of the district KANU branch in August-September 1966.[12] What seemed to have emerged at that time was a dominant-faction system,[13] in which Kiano himself could maintain a clear ascendancy over Mwaura and those he represented, but was not capable of destroying the Mwaura group altogether.

Apart from the Mwaura faction, however, Kiano had recruited political support in the other three divisions from different social groups, again on diverse principles—Kikuyu solidarity, the need to maintain access to government resources, fear of land confiscation or redistribution, political office, local patronage, and so forth. But, while it is true that the interests of these groups were identical (or were

[10] Ibid., p. 323.
[11] Nicholas, op. cit.
[12] See pp. 46-49 above.
[13] Graham op. cit., p. 324.

perceived to be, for the time being) in opposition to socialism as personified by Kaggia, it is also true that within the dominant faction there were (or could develop) groups with particular economic interests—particular models of the 'right' distribution of resources within a generally capitalist economic framework—which sharply conflicted with each other, and therefore with the aggregative assumptions of factional leaders which had developed in the struggle against Kaggia. In other words, if class consciousness developed along the lines implied in Kaggia's general programme, it would clearly mean the end of the sort of factions hitherto dominating Murang'a politics, since these factions rested on principles of political organization that presupposed no developed class consciousness or class-based political action. It will be suggested below that the activity of the Mwaura group in the coffee and co-operative disputes of 1967 furnished some evidence that such a trend was indeed taking place in Murang'a; it will also be necessary to set out later more general questions and reservations about the course of Kenyan politics and the political significance of social stratification in the Kikuyu countryside.

Aside from these general issues, however, there is the fact that there were in Murang'a very strong external political influences inhibiting such a breakdown in the existing factional system. Briefly, the centre deployed influences and controls—through KANU and through the Administration—which not only reinforced factional styles of conflict, but which imposed very high costs on potentially fissiparous political action. The regime was not only intolerant of the formation of new corporate political organizations (especially where the Kikuyu were concerned, as the experience of the KPU had demonstrated), but also developed a range of techniques for controlling and suppressing the overt expression of factional conflict itself.

These techniques were referred to in chapters 2 and 3—the denial by the Administration of a public platform for dissidents, the general increase in administrative powers to control local political activity (as in the extension of the power of chiefs), the prohibition of independent candidates for elections and the provision that candidates must be approved by a registered political party. In a more general sense, too, the regime could coerce politicians at the local level by the grant or denial of office or of government resources, and by demanding adherence to the ideological priorities which KANU had come to embody in the political struggles of 1964-66.

It is difficult to assess the longer-term effects of these centralizing tendencies: they would seem to inhibit overt political conflict in the rural areas, such as had taken place in the years immediately after independence, but only to the extent that they conferred advantages on politicians who already had access to leading figures in national politics or offices within the KANU hierarchy, and who could thereby hope to prevent local opponents from engaging in political competition through denial of the KANU label. Even before the introduction of legal provisions about party labels in April 1968, however, it is apparent that this was the party's central role: to confer the right to engage in political competition.[14] The party had not existed as an instrument of mass political participation since independence, and because of its organizational decay was not capable of acting either as a development agency (even assuming that the leadership would have wished it to) or as an instrument for exercising some degree of control over party leaders. What it could be used for, however, was to control political disintegration in the countryside and to decide who would be given access to political office and to the other tenures which party and State effectively controlled.

But the central government, of course, also had to make calculations about the cost of exercising control over local politics in particular situations, just as local politicians had to assess what the centre would tolerate. In Murang'a the national leadership was able to command compliance in settling the dispute over Kiano's leadership in August-September 1966; over the issue of coffee control in 1967, as we have seen, it was not. Part of the inability to do so in this situation lay in the fact that it anticipated adverse reactions to government attempts to enforce control (if it anticipated any) only in the generalized sense that coffee growers would not like the planting restrictions, and in this it reckoned without the political capacity of the group which has been termed, for the sake of brevity, the peasant leadership.

Rural Political Control

The Mwaura group in Kandara was dominated, as was suggested in chapter 3, by 'the rich, the powerful and the loyal'—men, such as Ndung'u Kagori and Jasmel Kariuki, who had benefited from the colonial regime not only in the sense that it provided them with government jobs, but because their opposition to Mau Mau during the Emergency had helped them to accumulate more land and greater wealth, or at the very least had enabled them to retain what they already possessed in a situation where a large number of people were being impoverished. In the factional struggles in the division and in the district, they had been joined by substantial numbers of rural traders and other entrepreneurs (some of whom, like Mwaura himself, were ex-detainees), but the rich-peasant element in the Mwaura group still predominated, and in large measure determined the issues and styles of

[14] This was, I think, what Kamau Njoroge had in mind when he told me: 'KANU exists to support itself'.

conservative politics in the division. While the activities of the nationalist movement in the early Sixties had at times challenged their predominance in Kandara society, the wealthier agriculturalists of the division had been able to accommodate nationalist demands and maintain control of a number of rural institutions.

Kaggia's nomination as KANU candidate for Kandara in 1963, and his assumption of the district KANU chairmanship in 1964, had deprived the Kandara rural leaders of their main political base: since 1960, they had controlled the party organization in the division, and Mwaura himself had been elected district chairman at the founding of the branch in 1961. Hence the formation of the Atiriri Bururi Union to oppose Kaggia in 1965, and hence the determination of the Kandara leaders to nominate Mwaura against Kaggia in the Little General Election, despite the very strong pressure from KANU headquarters.

The essential point is that the 'Mwaura faction', or rather the group which controlled it, was not merely a localized or geographically based entity, such as was Johnson Muigai's, for example.[15] It was also representative of a particular social and political group (and was thought to be so by the politicians in the district), more numerous and more powerful in Kandara than elsewhere in the district—because Kandara was the most developed of Murang'a divisions, and because the political and social cleavages of the Emergency had taken a more intense form in Kandara than elsewhere in the district. This is not to suggest that Mwaura was a mere figurehead, for he undoubtedly possessed some personal following of his own. Nevertheless, it is clear that the motives of the larger landowners were at all times the primary considerations, and that the other groups which gave allegiance to the faction were subordinate—rural transporters and traders were dependent on the wealthier peasants for custom and profit, and in any case were often peasant farmers in their own right as well.

The rural leadership had been able to retain control of the organizations they had operated—and in some cases established—during the Emergency. As was shown in chapter 4, former Home Guards and loyalists dominated the local school committees, which gave them an important advantage in gaining control of self-help groups when these were established after independence, since the school committees were most often the base on which CD committees were formed, and since so much of self-help was concerned with the provision of educational facilities. Their control of co-operatives, too, was never seriously challenged since—particularly after 1964—Kaggia's supporters included few farmers with enough land to grow much coffee and thereby be influential members of coffee societies.

The politicians who led the Mwaura faction were therefore in a

[15] See p. 31 above.

strong position to influence the allocation of development resources after independence. Whereas the Kiano group in the other divisions represented social groups with varying economic interests, the Kandara leadership which Mwaura represented could concentrate its resources on channelling benefits to a fairly restricted and well defined set of people.

Where community development was concerned, Kandara peasant leaders were able, despite the initial efforts of government officers to ensure 'non-political' communal efforts, virtually to monopolize representation on self-help committees, and thus to ensure that government counterpart funds (and the prestige associated with self-help projects) went to them and were denied their opponents.

On the coffee control issue, it was the same political group which had the resources and the direct economic interest to mobilize growers against the restrictions, whereas the KANU notables from the other divisions became involved in the struggle as a defensive response to the activism of the Kandara group.

The role of the Kandara leadership in the co-operative reform conflicts of 1967 cannot be seen in quite the same light though the interests of the richer peasants as a class were here no less clear cut. To the extent that the reforms involved a threat to their ability to control the co-operative societies in the division, the rich peasants were active participants in the anti-Union struggle. The co-operative societies not only offered the chance of extra income, through the malpractices described in Chapter 6, but also conferred status, political resources and favoured treatment for those in leading positions. Politically, the co-operatives had been used at times to recruit supporters in the political struggles in the division and, according to several informants, to provide funds for county council and parliamentary election campaigns: especially where the issues concerned land or 'free things', as they had done in the struggle against Kaggia; coffee growers, as those who had most to lose from any measures to 'correct Emergency injustices', could be counted on to provide active and on occasion violent support for the rural conservatives. In the past, too, the richer peasants who dominated the primary society committees had been able to secure preferential grading for their coffee cherry[16], although here again the transfer of graded staff to the Union had largely eliminated this advantage.

In short, control of the affairs of primary societies, like control of community development committees helped to preserve the dominance of wealthier farmers over the economic and political life of

---

[16] Cf. *Plan*, p. 198: '... committee members or their relatives demand top grading for inferior cherry, and society employees, holding their jobs at the committees' will, are not in a strong enough position to refuse.'

Kandara. Greater powers for the Union entailed closer supervision of primary society affairs by a government agency (which reduced the pecuniary advantages of co-operative leadership) and the removal of certain resources to an arena (the Union) over which the Kandara committee men did not have the same degree of control. The Kandara elite did not entirely succeed in defeating the reforms, as they had done in the case of coffee control. What they did do, however, was to delay the reforms in some cases and reduce their effectiveness in others. In their leadership of the struggle against restrictions, moreover, they secured for themselves clear predominance in the Union management committee, thus ensuring that the Union's role as government agent would be carefully circumscribed and primary societies left with as much local autonomy as possible.

Government development intentions in Murang'a were thus frustrated or modified in a number of important respects. Particularly where coffee planting control was concerned, a programme which was perceived at the time to be of major importance was effectively defeated by local politicians—with a specific group of richer farmers playing the critical role in that defeat. Government attempts at co-operative reform, seen as integral to the general need to extend State control over coffee production and marketing, were modified in a way which reflected the distribution of rural political power.

The ability of Murang'a politicians to intervene successfully in these programmes throws interesting light on the nature of power at the national level. The government had deliberately increased the powers of the Administration, and increasingly depended, as its colonial predecessors had done, on the Provincial and District Commissioners and their coercive apparatus to maintain political control of the countryside. Control over the party was being centralized, to ensure that the national elite could effectively control fissiparous tendencies at the local level, and to ensure that entry into political roles was carefully regulated.

The inability of government to resist the demands of local politicians that planting control should be ended demonstrated that this centralization of power was still subject to important constraints. Even though Kaggia and the KPU had been all but excluded from legitimate political competition, in Murang'a and in the country in general, the opposition nevertheless represented a threat to the national leadership which had to be contained. The coffee farmers constituted an influential section of support for the Kikuyu elite, and had demonstrated that they were capable of militant action in support of their demands. At the same time, the Kikuyu leaders who dominated KANU and government were not without challengers. The factional conflicts within KANU had by no means been extirpated with the departure of Odinga and the radicals in 1966[17], and there existed within the Kikuyu leadership a degree of tension (or rather varying degrees of loyalty to Kenyatta's 'court', although not to Kenyatta himself[18]) which had to be managed and controlled. With such influential members of the national leadership as Kiano having a strong influence in reversing the uprooting provisions and with prominent members of the rural Kikuyu establishment, such as Ndung'u Kagori, interceding directly with the President, the supposed economic necessities of control were overridden.

Planning and Rural Power

The Kenya Development Plan set out a strategy which assumed a basically capitalist economic structure; the plan, like its ideological underpinning, the Sessional Paper on African Socialism, accepted the economic system inherited from colonial times, and aimed at maximum expansion and rationalization within it. The most radical changes were planned or have occurred only where the most obvious discrimination or inequity existed—in the White Highlands and in alien domination of commercial life—and even there the solutions did not at all conflict with the Plan's free enterprise approach.[19]

In the field of agricultural development, the 'improvement approach' once more predominated, and the market orientation of the Plan was maintained: resources were to be concentrated in the areas of high productivity and (in the case of ranching schemes in pastoral areas) of immediate high potential.[20] Within the 'development areas', properly so called, resources would be further concentrated on the wealthier farmers. The clearest evidence of this is the rural credit programme

---

[17] See Gertzel, op. cit., chapter 2; Lamb, 'The Political Crisis in Kenya', op. cit.; and George Bennett, 'The Succession in Kenya', *The World Today*, August 1968.

[18] See Gertzel, op. cit., p. 17.

[19] For a convenient summary, see Judith Heyer, 'Kenya's Cautious Development Plan', *East Africa Journal*, August 1966. Ahmed Mohiddin's critique of Kenyan African Socialism ('Sessional Paper No. 10 Revisited', *East Africa Journal*, March 1969) is relevant here:

> Kenya African socialism is more of a case against the non-African incumbents of key positions in the economic and social structure, than a radical attempt to re-structure society, to create new values and institutions (p. 9). ... it is only laissez-faire capitalism that receives any serious critical appraisal, in fact praised for its adaptability. Modern capitalism is left untouched; capitalism as a socio-economic system is not that bad; all that is needed is more African involvement in the system (p. 12).

[20] See Heyer, 'Kenya's Agricultural Development Policy', *East African Economics Review*, Vol. 2, new series No. 2, December 1966, esp. pp. 44-5.

begun in late 1967 and extending over four years, providing £4.3m. to 'benefit only about 3% of Kenya's land-owning peasantry (excluding pastoralists); the 3% comprising, moreover, relatively progressive smallholders who are by definition already much better off than the rest'.[21] The basis of rural credit, and of successful agricultural development in general, was seen as the creation of a peasantry holding freehold and therefore secure and mortgageable title to its land—and no less than £4.36m. out of a total agricultural expenditure (excluding expenditure in connection with the former White Highlands) of £21.64m. was allocated to land consolidation and registration.[22]

In the rural areas, therefore, the Plan relied on the emerging wealthier farmers to effect the most marked development, assisted by extension, research and rural credit (but not significantly assisted by improved marketing facilities, the absence of which were a weak feature of the Plan). For the poorer peasants who did not qualify for development inputs, relative deprivation could be cushioned to some extent by the provision of rural amenities and social services—and at this point the community development programme assumed particular political importance since, as we have seen, the provision of local roads, water supplies, health dispensaries and other services was largely to be made by the peasants themselves, only minimally assisted by government.

Murang'a presented something of a special case in examining how these development choices worked out at the local level. The coffee planting restrictions were an unusual and interesting example of development policy in that they were designed to control production rather than to maximize it. Some expansion in the total crop was indeed envisaged, but not by way of bringing more land under coffee cultivation. The resources which were made available to expand production were those of the Coffee Authority, to build more processing facilities—and here, although there was some attempt on the part of the co-operative committee men to profit from factory building programmes, the expansion scheme was on balance seen as unfavourable to the growers, because it necessitated a further levy on their cash income and confusion over the repayment of loans.

The restrictive element in coffee policy, however, which from the growers' viewpoint was far more important. provoked the mobilization of political resources to protect growers' interests, and in the campaign which followed it was precisely that group of peasants which the government had identified as the vanguard of rural development which was instrumental in defeating government development policy. The same group also possessed the interests and the political capacity to

[21] *Plan*, p. 133.
[22] Calculated from *Plan*, pp. 127-8.

retain and extend their control of local institutions—co-operatives and community development committees—so as to preserve the economic and political advantages which flowed from control.

In this process, again, the 'rational' needs of development were superceded by what emerged as the reality of local political power. These tendencies, it is true, had been implicit in the political conflicts within KANU after independence, and later between KANU and KPU. The allocation of benefits between districts had been influenced by political as well as economic criteria, and within districts ideological cleavages had, after 1964, assumed critical importance. The nature of the Kandara group, however, and its effectiveness in controlling rural resources and preventing events which threatened its interests, seemed to indicate that even sharper political cleavages were beginning to have an effect on the distribution of resources—cleavages which had not hitherto been acknowledged in development policy-making, and which were the more effective for that. The bias in development policy in favour of the wealthier farmers had been modified by the promotion of an ethic of communal effort and sacrifice (and non-exploitation) exemplified, in practical terms, in the self-help programme. The indications in Murang'a, however, were that this device was of limited long-term usefulness: it would surely be optimistic to claim that the fact that Kandara self-help institutions, for example, were controlled by wealthier peasants did not mean that their political opponents (i.e. Kaggia's supporters, for the most part drawn from the poorest sections) would be denied the benefits—or at the very least, be compelled to buy them rather more dearly than would otherwise be the case.

The theme which emerges most strongly in these pages can be simply stated: that patterns of class formation and related patterns of political power had a marked effect on the implementation of specific development policies in Murang'a. The state's ability to exercise control or redirect resources to counter these tendencies was limited, despite a strongly centralized formal administrative and political apparatus, by the structure of political conflict at both national and district level, and by the ruling group's political obligations to the wealthier peasants.

The references to social class and stratification in this book, however, have not up to this point attempted to place the Murang'a evidence in a wider context, nor to construct a theory about the process of stratification in Kenya. The imprecise terminology in the foregoing discussion ('rural leadership', 'peasant elite', etc.) is enough indication that substantial uncertainties exist about the longer-term implications of the political conflicts described in these pages. Nevertheless, it is clearly important to consider the Murang'a evidence for the light that it throws on class and political change in Kenya as a whole, and to relate these considerations to ideas about peasant societies and African development which have a direct bearing on the matters discussed in this book.

Rural Development and Political Change

The development of ideological conflict and the rapid sequence of political changes in Murang'a in the period discussed in this study represented, in a sense, a phase of re-evaluation of the criteria of power and status in rural society at a time—around independence—of considerable uncertainty.

Plainly, the British withdrawal prompted general uncertainties in Kenyan life, some of which—about the regional and ethnic distribution of power—had found political expression in KADU's existence. Where Murang'a in particular was concerned, the issue was one of translating the general myths of the independence movement into concrete terms more relevant to the conditions of rural life. Given that African government was assured, a number of subsidiary questions—about land, jobs, education—confronted Kenyans. What rules would the newly-Africanized centre apply in allocating these prizes? How were politicians and their supporters to assure a flow of benefits?

In this state of flux, politicians in Murang'a in this period can be seen as offering alternative political languages—competing criteria of social and political status—as solutions to these problems. Where the independence movement had for the most part assumed an undifferentiated African mass, its assumption of power made it necessary for politicians to attempt to elaborate such criteria. That this sort of competition was particularly sharp in Murang'a is not very surprising. Whereas non-Kikuyu areas were primarily concerned to see that their areas were not altogether left out of account, the Kikuyu could be reasonably assured of both government resources and access to political patronage: the problem was one of determining who was going to get these resources within the Kikuyu localities themselves.

The history of Murang'a during colonial times had been one of quite sharp social and political cleavages, cleavages closely related to the social structure of the district; there was thus a tradition of social conflict which was not nearly so marked in other areas of Kenya. This does not of course imply that the Murang'a situation differed fundamentally from that obtaining elsewhere, but it remains true that the peculiar features of relatively advanced development, sharp historic social conflicts and weak traditional social organization combine to set Murang'a somewhat apart from many other areas of Kenya. At the same time, however, it is true that to the extent that other districts successfully develop along similar agricultural lines, as government policy would suggest, they may be expected to be vulnerable to many of the social and political influences which we have seen at work in Murang'a.

Murang'a leaders extended these conflicts into the independence period either by trying to institutionalize older political criteria or by defining new ones, in each case legitimizing their cases by reference to KANU's nationalist themes: in Kaggia's case, the argument was that entitlement to the benefits of nationalist government was, initially at least, to be coterminous with participation in or support for the Mau Mau movement a proposition soon elaborated and extended in the more 'class-conscious' terms of rich versus poor. Similarly Kiano sought to invoke nationalist themes, but in a manner which was much closer to the 'official' line set out in the Sessional Paper on African Socialism—i.e. an assertion of the advantages of individual enterprise and the dangers of radical or socialist policies, and with minimal stress on social divisions apart from commonplace assertions about the need to redistribute income through welfare policies lest the gap become harmfully wide. Kiano's ideological position bore a close relationship to the spread of his political support among various sections of the rural community, as we have seen: likewise Mwaura's rather more robust championing of the Protestant ethic reflected the interests of the group he represented.

In this activity Murang'a leaders were, to a significant extent, anticipating social and economic changes in their identification of specific social groups as having particular political interests. In rapidly changing circumstances interests could and did change (for example in the defections from Kaggia's camp in 1965-66), or social groups might themselves become socially or politically marginal (landless ex-detainees are perhaps an example) either in the sense of being unable to exert significant political power, or because changes in the peasant economy and society have made their very existence as a group problematical. There is also the point, of course, which has been made about Odinga: that the use of socialist rhetoric (which naturally tends to produce a complementary, opposing, rhetoric from opponents) is a useful tactic of factional leaders in political infighting, devoid of specific socio political importance.

There are powerful arguments of consistency, and of group interests, in the Murang'a case, which militate against such a simple explanation: indeed, the 'factional politics' and the 'class' argument meet, as has been suggested here, at the point where politicians discern that class or class-like principles are a potential method of recruiting support. The political conflicts in Murang'a were thus not merely a matter of competing languages and symbols: there existed, as we have seen, fairly clear and self-conscious social cleavages which took the form of embryonic class conflict. The problem, therefore, is one of assessing the immediate and longer-range importance of these class divisions in the Kikuyu countryside.

Clearly the class divisions have up to now been contained within the limits of KANU's domination of political life. It is plain that Kaggia continued to be regarded as a major threat to KANU's control in the Kikuyu political hinterland: in late 1967 he and his wife were badly beaten while visiting Thika, in what was plainly a political assault. The following year he was sentenced to a term in prison for addressing an illegal meeting in the district, and the KPU Murang'a office, after having been wrecked by a crowd led by Kiano in July 1967, was never allowed to function normally. But if this was evidence that the KPU's attacks on the political elite and the wealthy were having some impact in Murang'a, it was a development which was cut short by the political upheavals of 1969.

In the wake of the murder of Tom Mboya in June, and the furious reaction of the Luo people, the Kikuyu were turned in on themselves, so to speak, in a manner in some ways reminiscent of the Emergency, in its emphasis on traditional values and Kikuyu chauvinism. Mboya's assassination provoked the Luos to the angriest reaction, but it also provided evidence of the popular dissatisfaction among other tribes with the Kikuyu-dominated KANU concensus. Certainly the Kikuyu leadership felt themselves to be faced with a major crisis of political control. In the months following the assassination, loyalty oaths were systematically administered to Kikuyu in towns and rural areas, accompanied at times by violence against recalcitrants. The power of this invocation of ethnic solidarity (taking the same form as the oathing of the Emergency, when the Kikuyu felt themselves to be comparably threatened) can be gauged from the fact that in August 1969 Kaggia himself announced that he had resigned as vice-president of the KPU and rejoined KANU. Thus the most bitter and enduring rift in the Kikuyu political ranks was symbolically healed in the face of what was seen as a threat to Kikuyu primacy.

The elections which followed a few months after the banning of the KPU in October 1969 confirmed that the ideological and social cleavages which had earlier been apparent in Murang'a were not now in evidence in political competition—although this is not to say, of course, that they no longer existed as politically significant facts. The December poll was in fact a KANU primary election, but effectively had the status of a general election since, with the opposition banned, no second stage of polling would be involved. Murang'a followed the pattern of many other parts of the country in that two out of five of the district's MP's were defeated, in both cases by relative newcomers to Murang'a politics.

In Kigumo, Kariuki Njiiri was relegated to second last of five candidates. The winner was Dr James Munene, repairing the setback to his political fortunes in Thika, who won 10,654 votes, a margin of 7,000 over his nearest opponent. In Kandara, Mwaura lost his seat to G. Mwichigi, a Kandara-born, Canadian-educated employee of the East African Community, and, with 2,575 votes, came second last of the five in the poll. Kaggia was second in the Kandara contest, with 5,520 votes, losing to the victor by 1,209. Gachago and Wanjagi held their seats by narrow majorities, but Kiano, in the Mbiri constituency, routed his four opponents (including Geoffrey Kebatta) by 14,287 to his nearest rival's 1,317.

To the extent that a consistent pattern can be discerned in the voting in Murang'a, it appears that considerations of district bargaining and local benefits were uppermost: thus Kiano, as the man who 'had the ear of *Mzee*', and had established himself as the virtually unchallengeable boss of KANU in the district, triumphed decisively, while Njiiri, although an Assistant Minister, seems to have been seen as merely Kiano's client. Munene, on the other hand, was very wealthy and had been prominent not only in Thika's municipal and KANU affairs, but in business in Murang'a itself; his education and status, like that of Mwichigi, the Kandara victor, evidently made a considerable impact.

The characteristic Kenyan pattern of regional and ethnic rivalry for government-controlled resources thus seemed to have been repeated at the constituency level. The Kikuyu had secured themselves against external threats by their communal solidarity and the suppression of political opposition; within the Kikuyu areas, now, they were concerned to maximize the effectiveness of their claims on government benefits. The critical factor which seemed for the time being to have halted the tendency toward polarization in Murang'a was the influence of the centre, as an authoritative source of symbols and norms about politics and the structure of society, and by the way in which it exercised power and disbursed resources to inhibit radical political expression and control internal conflict in local politics. Ultimately, the challenge presented by Kaggia's radicalism could be effectively absorbed: in the crisis of 1969, the Kikuyu leadership was able to externalize discontent by invoking an ethnic rather than a class interest in the continuation of the Kikuyu-dominated elite's political control.

That the elite was able to do so has much to do with the relative lack of overtly exploitative relationships in the peasant areas. As the analysis of the Murang'a social order indicates, the wealthier peasants are not very obviously in the position of exploiters of the small and marginal peasants—or, what is more important, are not perceived as such. Their privileged access to rural wealth, and to resources flowing into the rural areas from outside, is more dependent on control over or preferential

Index

Little General Election, 23, 24, 40, 44-6, 67, 112, 139
Luo, 17, 20, 21n, 23, 24, 147

Maendelo ya Wanawake (Progress for Women), 56
Mahugu, Kabiri, 101n
Majimbo (regionalism), 18, 24, 33
Majimbo Constitution, 17
Mau Mau, 8, 10-11, 13, 28, 31, 44, 138, 146
mbari, 8, 11, 14
Mboya, T J, 10n, 18, 20-22, 28, 30, 37, 44, 62-3, 147
McKenzie, B, 106
Middleton, J, 8n
Million Acre Scheme, 103
Mituikire, 31-2
Mohiddin, A, 142n
Moore, B, 2n
Mshugu, Kabiri, 65n
Muigai, Johnson, 29, 30-31, 35, 42-3, 139
Munene, James, 51, 148
Mungai, Njoroge, 20
Munoko, N W, 48
Murang'a Farmers Co-operative Union, 88-106, 113-30, 140-41
Muruka Coffee Growers Co-operative Society, 95
Mwangi, Kiiru, 35, 39
Mwaura, Taddeo, 28, 30-45, 48, 51, 65-8, 70-71, 77-8, 80, 97-8, 101, 112, 123, 125-26, 136-40, 148
Mweru, Kamau, 32, 39
Mwichigi, G, 148

national elite, 1, 4, 19, 25, 38, 148, 150-51
Ndung'u, F, 97
Ngala, R, 20-21, 111
Ngei, P, 18, 36
Nginda Society, 97
Nicholas, R W, 3, 36n
Njiiri, Kariuki, 16, 28, 30, 35, 38-9, 48-9, 100, 147
Njonjo, C, 20-21
Njonjo, J M, 51
Njoroge, Kamau, 33n, 38n, 42n, 47-9, 72, 77, 101, 107, 125-26, 138n
Nottingham, J, 18n
Nyagah, J, 21n

oathing, 25, 147
Odede, W, 18
Odinga, Oginga, 10n, 18, 20-23, 30, 35, 38, 41-2, 142, 146
Okelo-Odongo, T, 20-21
Oneko, A, 20-21
Operation Anvil, 11
Oxenham, J, 54n

personal discount system, 115, 119
Pinto, P, 20
primary societies, 87, 91-2, 95, 100, 103, 108, 112, 115-25, 128-31, 140-41
Prosser, A R G, 54n

Regional Assemblies, 18, 33
Registration Act, 15
Rosberg, C, 8n, 10n
Rural Credit Programme, 142-43

Sanger, C, 18n
Saul, J, 2n, 3n
Schaffer, B B, 54n
Self Help, 37, 54-60, 63-5, 69-81, 139, 140, 144
Sessional Paper on African Socialism, 74, 142, 146
Shanin, T, 2n
Sorrenson, M P K, 8n, 11n, 12n, 13n, 14, 132
Suspension of Suits Acts, 15

Tanzania African National Union (TANU), 20
Thabuni, Mwangi, 29, 34, 37, 38n, 48-9, 68, 98-9, 125
Thuku, Harry, 6
Thungu, Arthur Wanyoike, 51

uprooting, 85-6, 92, 95-6, 98-100, 102, 106-08, 125-26

Van Arkadie, B, 150
villagization, 11, 12

Wahome, W, 55-6, 71-9
Wainana, J, 35
Waiyaki, F L M, 21n
Wanjagi, R Mwangi, 39-41, 48-9, 101, 125, 148
Wanyoike, Mburu, 43
Wasserman, G, 5n, 19

Waweru, G, 97-8
Waweru, Kihara, 34n
Williams, J, 120
Wolf, E, 2n

Wood, R, 2n
Wrigley, C C, 7n, 8n

youth centres, 59

KENYA: indicating tribal
location of MURANG'A dis[trict]
and the Abedare Range

KANGEMA DIVISION

Sagana

FOREST DIVISION

● Kangema

Kiharu ●
● Mura

KIHARU DIVISION

● Kigumo

KIGUMO DIVISION

KANDARA DIVISION

● Kandara

● Makuyu

MURANG'A DISTRICT

0   4   8
scale in miles
trunk road ▬▬

● Thika

↙ To Nairobi